W9-ANJ-695

MEL BAY'S COMPLETE BASS BOOK

BY MIKE HILAND

CD CONTENTS*

*This book is available as a book only or as a book/compact disc configuration.

This book is available either by itself or packaged with a companion audio and/or video recording. If you have purchased the book only, you may wish to purchase the recordings separately. The publisher strongly recommends using a recording along with the text to assure accuracy of interpretation and make learning easier and more enjoyable.

1 2 3 4 5 6 7 8 9 0

Visit us on the Web at www.melbay.com — E-mail us at email@melbay.com

Table of Contents

Foreword

Hello fellow bass players! This book is intended to be an A–Z guide for intermediate to advanced bass players. That means that we skip some of the basics and get into some of the more detailed aspects of playing bass. I hope that, by going through this book, you will learn some new things, find answers to old questions, and even come up with some new questions. Questions like "What else can I do?" are my favorite. After being shown some new ideas, that is the question I always ask myself.

In this book I hope to share with you things that I have learned from experience as well as those things that we learn in classes, music books, even interviews and conversations with other players. We all play music at different levels of professionalism. Some do nothing but play music, while others can't seem to find enough time to play because of other responsibilities. Because of this, I have tried to include information that can be used whether you're playing in a garage band or doing studio work.

Bass playing has come a long way in the past few years and will continue to grow in the future. That means that its role is becoming more complex. This requires a greater knowledge and understanding of the instrument and its role in contemporary music. This book will help you break the ice and begin exploring new concepts in bass playing right away, from new playing techniques like right-hand hammering to understanding scales and chord tones and how they can be used in developing bass lines. So, dive right in and start playing!

Once again I'd like to give a big "thank you" to Mr. William Bay and everyone at Mel Bay Publications for making these books a reality! Thanks to Jeff Marsh for his valued input, and to George and Gloria Kaye and the staff at Kaye's Music Scene. This book is dedicated to Dorothy for all her love and support in the creation of this book. I really appreciate everyone's help and support!

Have Fun!

......Mike

Exercises

The first thing we should talk about is proper right- and left-hand technique. First, I will provide some basic "rules" for proper hand placement and playing technique. The player should then apply these rules to the exercises and musical examples found in all sections of this book.

Be aware that we must use the term "rules" loosely. These rules are ideas that have been found to be very beneficial and common among many of the finer players. You should take these rules as constructive suggestions and try them out. The most important thing to remember is that, no matter what technique you choose, it should be comfortable and lend itself to your playing style.

LEFT-HAND TECHNIQUE ....

Smooth and efficient left-hand techniques are essential to good playing. It is very important to both the tone and feel of the music that you are playing to be able to play the necessary notes smoothly, accurately, and with the right touch. Here are the important things to remember about left-hand technique:

1. The left-hand fingers should lie lightly across the strings and must *always* be relaxed. If your hand is stiff or tense, you will not be able to move your fingers easily, making it difficult to move smoothly, quickly, and accurately.

2. The left-hand fingers should be spread out slightly so that each finger covers one fret all the way across all four strings. Again, your whole hand should be relaxed.

3. The left thumb should rest against the back of the neck, lining up with the space between the index and second fingers. The thumb should make contact with the neck just below the midpoint of the back of the neck. (If your neck has a stripe running the length of it, use that as a guide, your thumb making contact with the bottom edge of the stripe.)

    NOTE: Never let your left thumb come up over the top of the neck. If you're grabbing it like a baseball bat, how are your going to move your hand quickly and smoothly up and down the neck?

Got all that? OK, let's place the left hand on the neck:

Lay your left-hand fingers across the strings so that each finger can cover one fret all the way across all four strings. (If your hands are smaller, it is OK to pivot your thumb so you can reach the E-string; just make sure your fingers stay flat and relaxed.) Now, keeping your hand relaxed, bring your left thumb around the back of the neck and position it between the first and second fingers, just below the midpoint of the radius of the neck. You're not squeezing or straining, are you?

Can your four left-hand fingers play four notes on the E-string in this position? Is it comfortable? If this is new to you, it may take a little while for your hand to get used to it. Practicing every day will help you get more comfortable with this technique.

RIGHT-HAND TECHNIQUE ....

1.   Anchor the right thumb either on a pick-up or on the low string on the bass. Anchoring the thumb in this way counterbalances the picking force of the right-hand fingers.

2.   Picking is done with the first and second right-hand fingers. The important thing to remember is always alternate the fingers in this order: 1-2-1-2-1-2.... It is very easy to get lazy and play simple parts with just the first finger, but **BEWARE!!** It's bad habits like this that will kill you in the long run. And, believe me, it *ain't no fun* to go back and overcome this bad habit!

     Even when picking across the strings, always alternate the right-hand fingers. In the exercises and examples in this book, as well as your day-to-day playing, pay very close attention to your right-hand picking technique.

3.   After a right-hand finger has picked a note, it should come back and touch the string below the string it just picked (after playing a note on the A-string, the right-hand finger should touch the E-string). When playing on the lowest string, let the finger come back and touch the right thumb (if it's not too far). Doing this with the right-hand fingers allows your fingers to subconsciously "know" where the strings are.

PLAYING WITH A PICK ....

Another way to pick the strings on the bass is to use a **pick.** When playing with a pick, use a "heavy" one because bass strings are very heavy, and thin picks will bend under the pressure, resulting in a weak attack on each picked note. (It should be noted that in some playing situations, that "weak attack" may be the desirable tone!) Here is the technique of playing with a pick:

1.   Hold the pick between the thumb and first finger so that it points in a 90-degree angle from the direction of the fingers (pointing directly towards the body of the bass).

2.   Pick the strings using a "down stroke" (across the string towards the floor). Pick only one string at a time. To pick the next note, use an "up stroke" (across the string towards the ceiling). Always alternate down stroke, up stroke, down stroke, up stroke, etc....

3. You can use the heel of the right hand to "mute" the strings back by the bridge. This is a very common technique in rock bass playing. One benefit of this technique is that it keeps unwanted notes from ringing.

DIAGRAMS USED IN THIS BOOK ....

In addition to written music, the two following types of diagrams will be used to help you identify where to play each piece. While the fret positions shown should be followed, the given fingerings are recommended fingerings. You are free to use your own fingerings within the fret positions shown, but I recommend that you try mine first, as they will help reinforce the right- and left-hand techniques described earlier.

TAB diagrams are common tablature, a form of musical notation primarily used by non-reading players. **Fretboard diagrams** are designed to help communicate ideas in this book. Here is how to read each type of diagram:

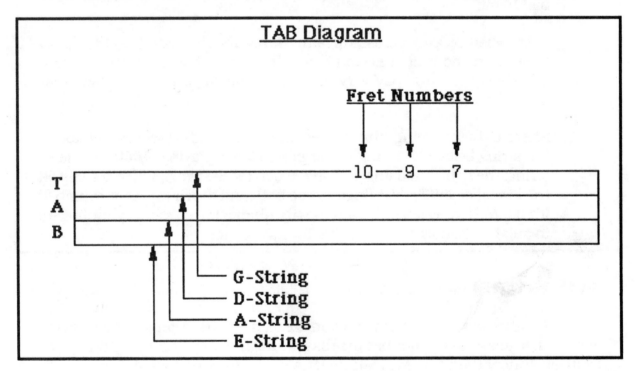

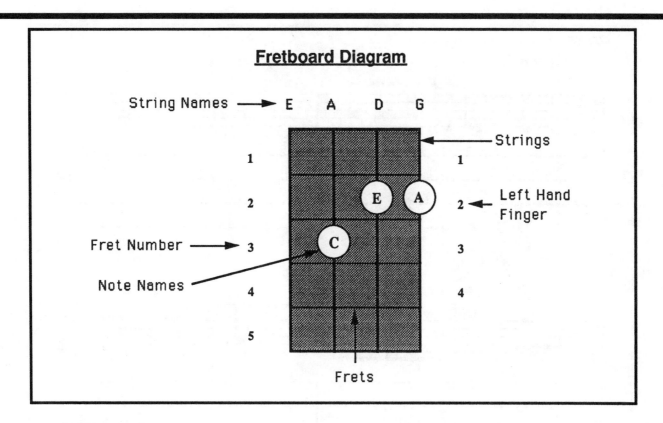

Fretboard Diagram

EXERCISES ....

Exercises are not meant to take the place of playing music. The best way to improve your playing is to play in "real" musical situations (i.e., recording and live gigs). Realistically, not all of us are working every day, and many of us are not professional musicians. Therefore, the opportunities may be limited. That is where exercises come into play. Use them to keep up your ability to play the parts that you will want to play.

This section contains a number of exercises designed to test and strengthen your right- and left-hand technique. They cover a wide variety of playing scenarios such as chromatic, cross-string, stretch (extended fingering), pedal-tone, and two-finger playing techniques. I recommend that you always play these exercises with a metronome or drum machine to develop and ensure good time-keeping habits.

Each exercise is shown in both written music and tablature form. Note that recommended left-hand fingerings are shown above the written music. Throughout this exercise section, I strongly urge you to use the recommended fingerings, as each exercise is designed to emphasize a specific fingering. Also, remember to use the "good" right- and left-hand technique habits previously discussed! Now, let's exercise.......

Exercise 1

Exercise 2

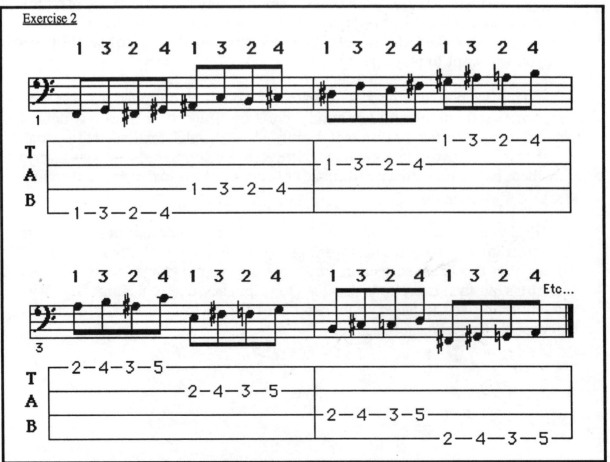

Exercise 3

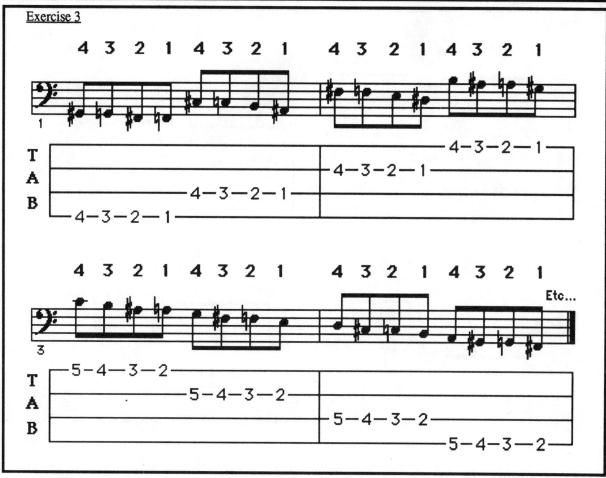

Exercise 4

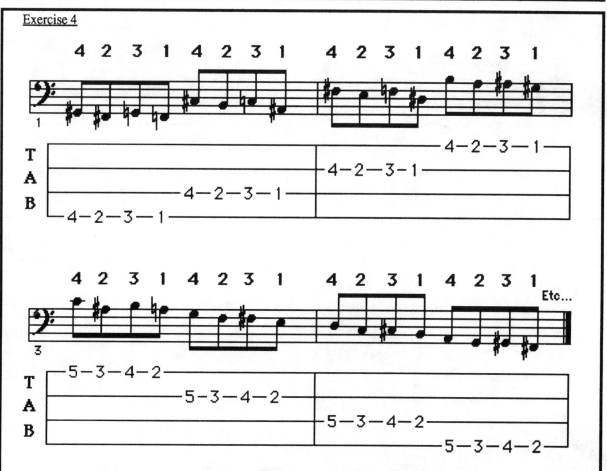

Exercise 5

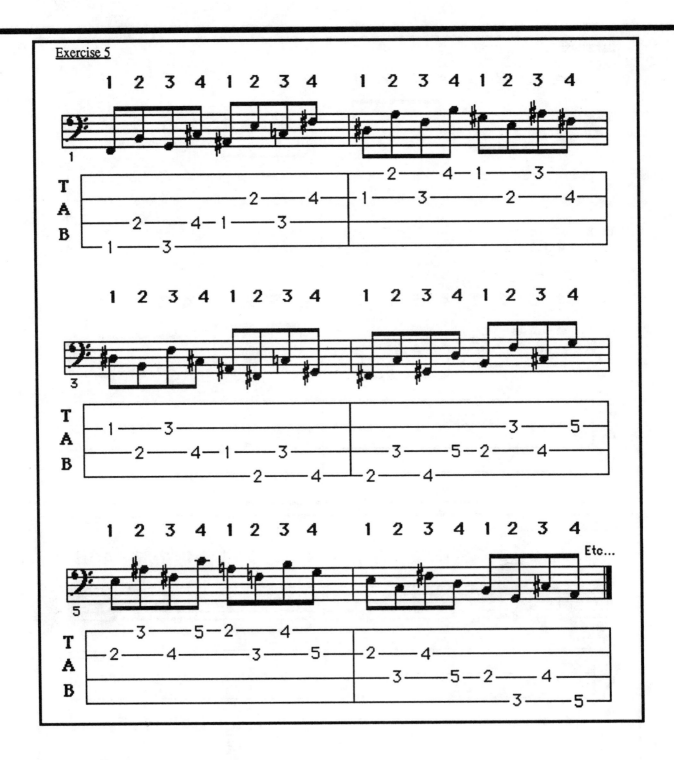

Exercise 6

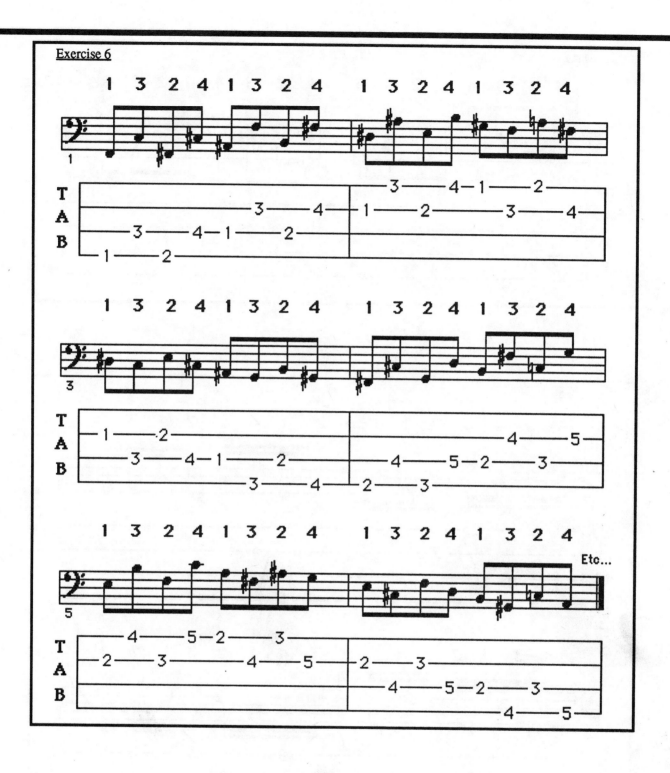

Exercise 7

Exercise 8

Exercise 9

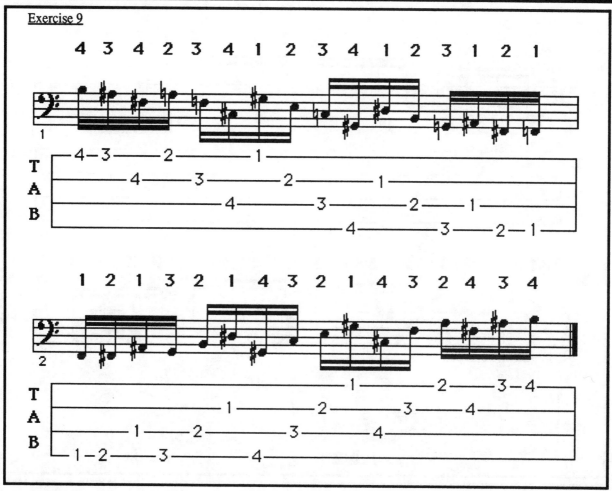

Exercise 10

Exercise 11

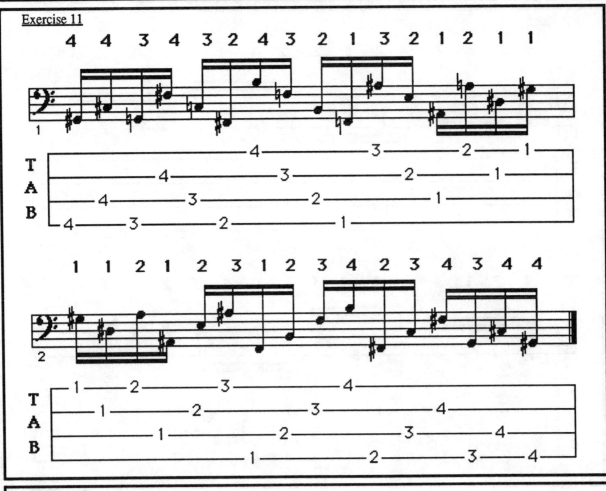

Exercise 12

Exercise 13

Exercise 14

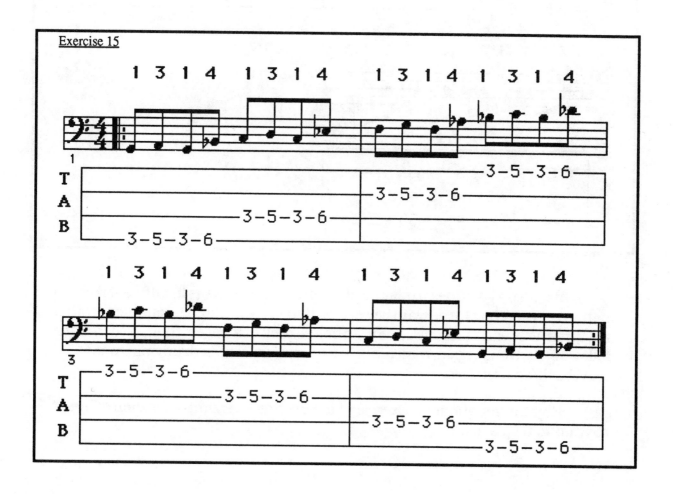

Exercise 15

This last exercise shows a left-hand fingering that uses only the first and second left-hand fingers. Play this exercise again using the second and third fingers, and then again using the third and fourth to fully benefit from it.

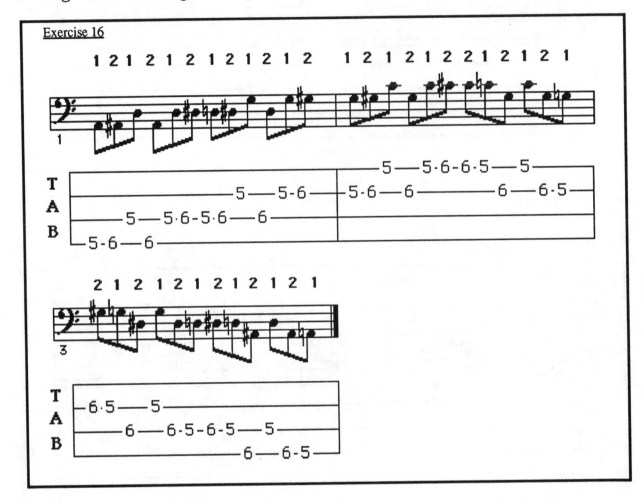

Exercise 16

It is also a good idea to play all of the previous exercises in different rhythm patterns in addition to the way they are written. Here are some examples of other rhythms. Play each exercise as written on the previous pages, then in each of the following rhythms. Again, remember to use a metronome or drum machine when playing these exercises.

Rhythm variations on Exercise 1 are used as an example for each different rhythm to be played.

Exercise Rhythm Variation 1

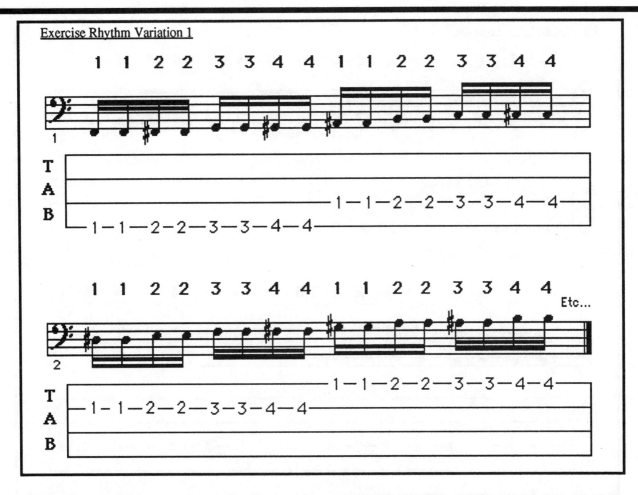

Exercise Rhythm Variation 2

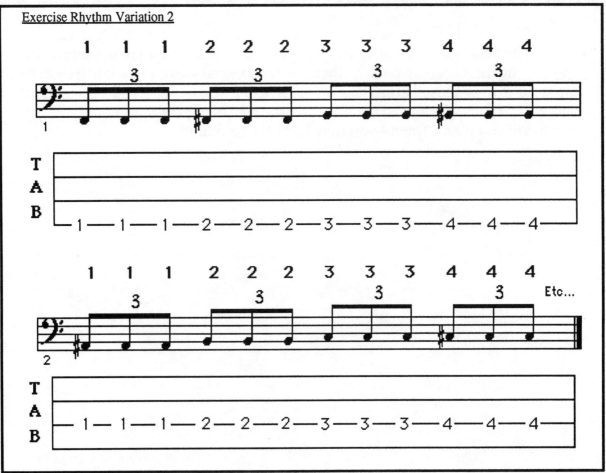

17

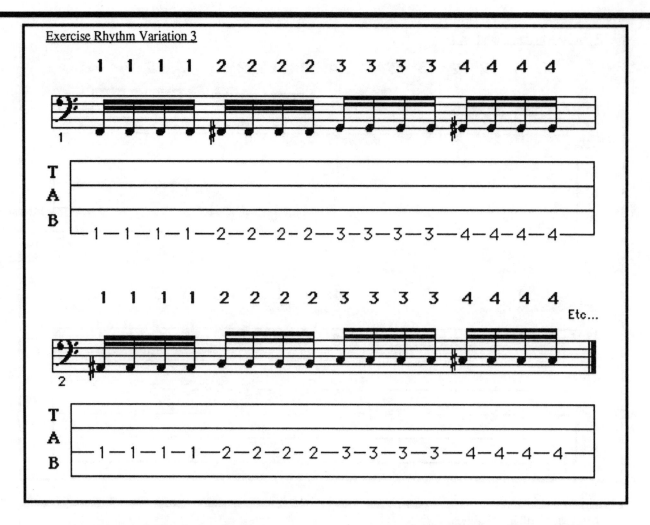

Exercise Rhythm Variation 3

This concludes the section on exercises. While all are certainly useful and should be practiced regularly, you will probably find that there are a few that benefit you most. I would pick out those five or six exercises and make up a warm-up routine to be played *every time you pick up the bass*. But, by all means, don't forget to go back and test yourself on all of the others regularly. After all, you paid me to tell you about them—you may as well use them!!

Reading

This book will not attempt to teach you how to read music. Instead, I am going to try to help you improve your reading abilities through numerous rhythmic and musical examples. Assuming you already know how to read notes on the staff, we will work through exercises on quarter, eighth, and sixteenth notes and rests; as well as quarter, eighth, and sixteenth triplets, ties in eighth- and sixteenth-note patterns, and some work with syncopated rhythm patterns.

There will also be musical examples of bass lines utilizing a number of these rhythm figures. And, finally, the ultimate test: sight reading. Sounds like we have a lot of work to do, so let's get to it....

RHYTHM STUDIES

I often draw similarities between reading music and reading the English language. Have you ever noticed that, when you are reading a book, you can read quickly through simple words and have to slow down for longer, more complicated words? Well, I have! I have also found through my personal playing and teaching experience that most people are the same when it comes to reading music.

If you are a decent reader of music, you will breeze through those quarter-note passages and may even be able to "ace" the eighth-note patterns. But, when you hit those syncopated sixteenth-note figures, it's time to run for cover!

OK, maybe you're not that bad. But, my bet is that you reach a point in your reading ability where you have to struggle. Why is that? Simple. You don't practice the more complicated rhythm figures. Well, I hope to change that.

Written music tells you two things: 1) which note to play and 2) how long to play that note. What if you had to *really think* only about one of those two things? The work of reading music would essentially be cut in half, wouldn't it? By studying rhythm figures to the point of recognizing what a given figure sounds like just at a glance, the only thing left to concentrate on is which note is to be played. Remember what I said about reading simple words quickly? Well, we want to increase your vocabulary of "simple words" to include as many eighth-note and sixteenth-note rhythm figures as possible. That way, you only have to think about *which* note is to be played.

To do this, we're going to need a lot of rhythm examples. Since we are studying rhythm, the note(s) played are not important. The examples all use the same note. I'm sure you wouldn't get arrested if you chose to use a different note or combination of notes than those that I have written. It is very important that each example is played with a metronome or drum machine and that each rhythm figure is repeated until you know it absolutely stone cold. To kid yourself is to sell yourself short of what you are really capable. So, make sure you really know each rhythm before moving on to the next. Enough talk, let's get busy....

First, let's take a look at some quarter notes. Fire up the metronome and try to read straight through. If you're thinking that quarter notes are no big deal, well let me remind you that it would sure be embarrassing if your "crash-and-burn" point came as early as quarter notes! Do not underestimate their importance.

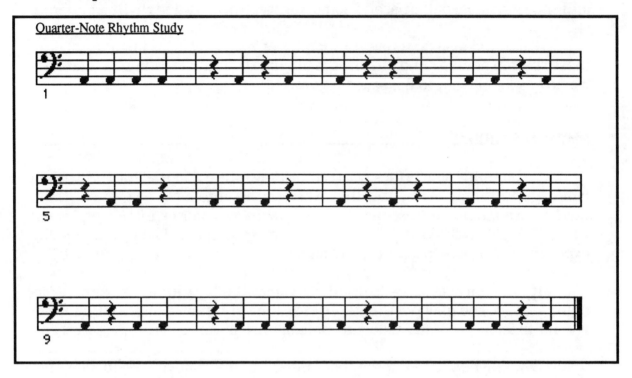

Next, we'll take a look at some eighth-note rhythms. In this example, it is important to get the feel for eighth notes in different parts of a measure. Be sure you understand what it feels like to play the eighth notes on the third beat, or the second beat, or first or fourth. Each feels a little different; understanding this will help you breeze right through most eighth-note passages.

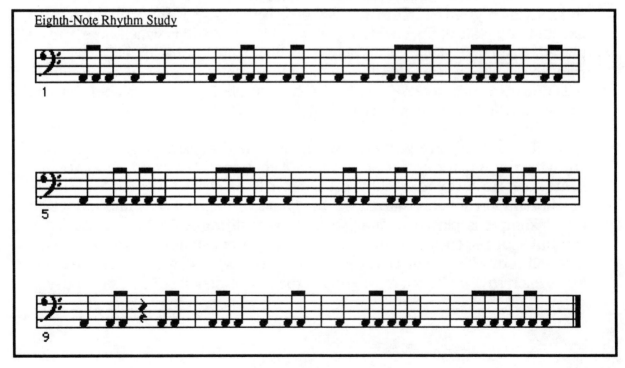

While quarter-note and eighth-note rhythm figures are primarily looked at one measure at a time, sixteenth-note rhythm figures can be looked at *one beat at a time*. In fact, there are five different sixteenth-note rhythm figures that could occupy one beat.

Therefore, we will emphasize sixteenth-note rhythms from a "single-beat" standpoint. In the next example, all five sixteenth-note rhythms are shown, and I have included the counting of the beats with the examples. Practice each different rhythm figure *one at a time* until you have a good grasp of how they are played *relative to a single beat*. Be sure to use a metronome and **count out loud** to help see and hear where the notes fall relative to the beats.

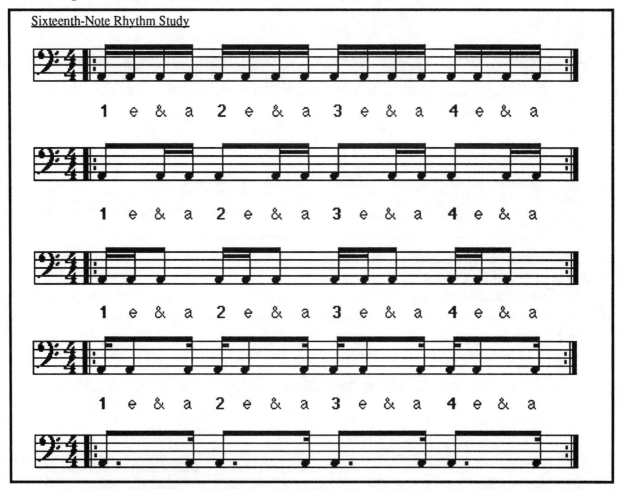

Sixteenth-Note Rhythm Study

I don't want to nag, but be sure that you can play any of the above rhythms at "first glance" before moving on. These rhythms are often tricky, and the examples in this book are only going to get more complicated, so make sure you can play them with no problem. 'Nuff said....

Now that we know these rhythms inside and out, let's try combining them within a measure. In fact, we're going to combine them in lots of measures! Here is a sixteenth-note exercise that uses all of the above rhythm figures.

HINT: If you get confused on the counting, I suggest that you write down the counting as shown above for each beat that gives you trouble.

Here are a couple of examples using eighth-note and sixteenth-note **rests.** Be sure that you do not have any note(s) ringing when you should be resting. An eighth note followed by a sixteenth rest is *not* the same as a dotted eighth note!

Triplets are next. To play triplets is to play three notes in the same amount of time as two notes of the same value. Eighth-note triplets indicate that you play three notes, equally spaced, in the time normally allotted for two eighth notes (or one beat). Quarter- and sixteenth-note triplets have similar definitions. Here are some examples of all three types of triplets.

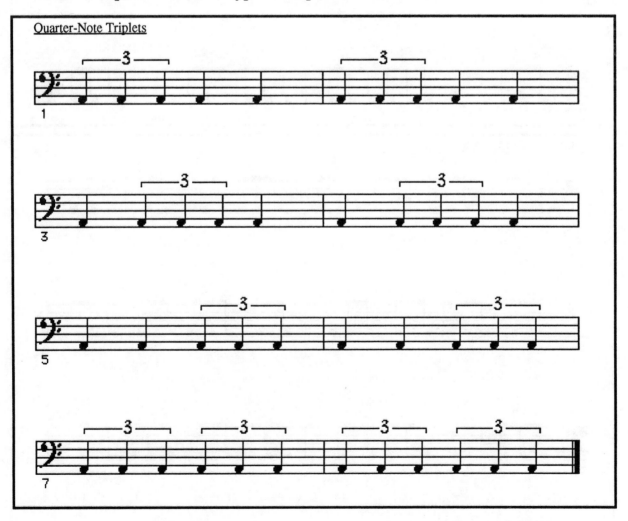

Eighth-Note Triplet Ex 1

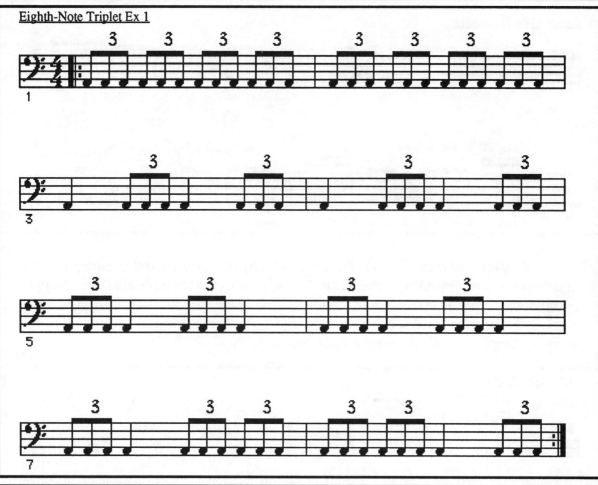

Eighth-Note Triplet Ex 2

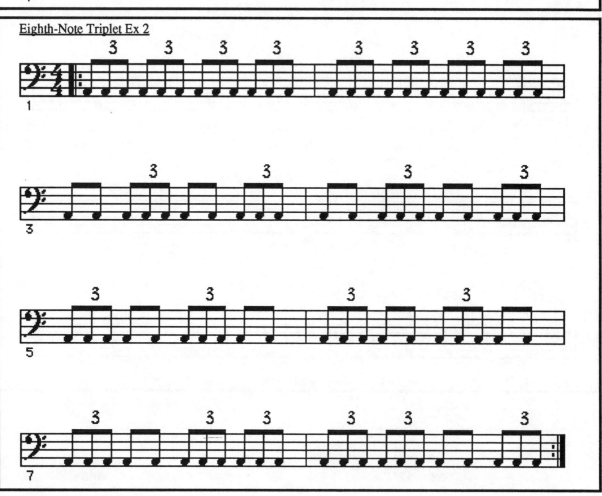

Sixteenth-Note Triplets

Ties are often used simply to confuse you and throw you off beat. At least that's how it seems sometimes, doesn't it? We will take a look at ties in eighth-note rhythm figures and then sixteenth-note rhythms.

If you understand and are able to handle eighth-note rhythm patterns, then ties in eighth-note figures probably won't confuse you too much. (No, that doesn't mean you don't have to practice them!!) As usual, though, sixteenth notes are a different breed of cat.

When there are ties in sixteenth-note rhythm figures, you are expected to hold notes for some fraction of a beat longer. Depending on the tempo, that can be really tricky! The way to approach this study is to look at each of the five different sixteenth-note rhythm figures studied earlier and how they may be tied to each other. This results in quite a number of different combinations.

As with the previous studies, it is a good idea to familiarize yourself with each two-beat rhythm figure (with ties) and add those to your "vocabulary." That way, when you are confronted with these tied rhythm figures, you will be able to breeze right through them as if they were half notes!

Eighth-Note Tie Study

Sixteenth-Note Tie Study Ex 1

Repeat each Measure 4 times.

Sixteenth-Note Tie Study Ex 2

Repeat each Measure 4 times.

Now it's time to start combining all of these quarter-, eighth-, and sixteenth-note rhythm figures into a few exercises. Having talked about a number of different rhythms, with and without the use of ties, we can now play around with the idea of **syncopation.** Syncopation basically means that the accents are on off-beats—not necessarily the middle of the beat, but anywhere within the beat except the downbeat. These next four exercises should expose you to the idea of syncopation and give you a little test in our rhythm studies. (Now is the time to start looking for some of the rhythm figures we have added to your vocabulary and see how well you recognize them.)

Eighth-Note Syncopation Ex 1

Eighth-Note Syncopation Ex 2

Sixteenth-Note Syncopation Ex 1

Sixteenth-Note Syncopation Ex 2

OK, I know!! We're sick of all of these one-note exercises!! Here are some examples of bass lines using different rhythm figures (and different notes!) to practice our new vocabulary of rhythm figures. Remember to use a metronome, and don't be embarrassed to count out loud with the beat. I would recommend starting out with a slow tempo. You may even want to kick the metronome up to a very quick tempo and let each beat of the metronome be equal to one sixteenth note in the exercise. Practice each exercise until you can fall into the "groove" created by the rhythm figures.

Rhythm Studies Ex 1

Rhythm Studies Ex 2

Rhythm Studies Ex 3

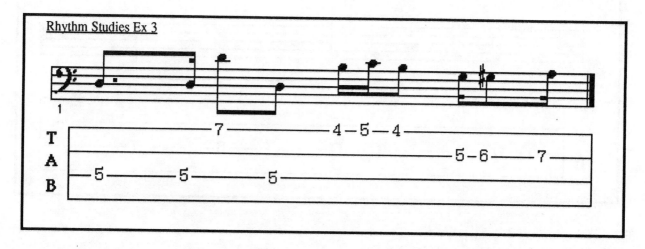

Rhythm Studies Ex 4

Rhythm Studies Ex 5

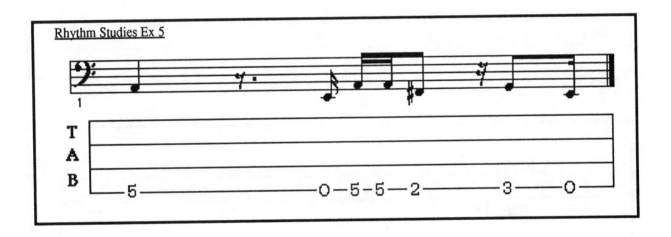

Rhythm Studies Ex 6

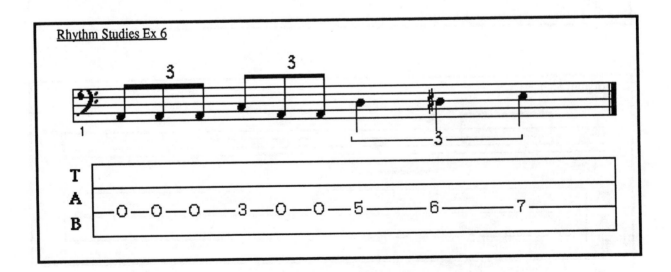

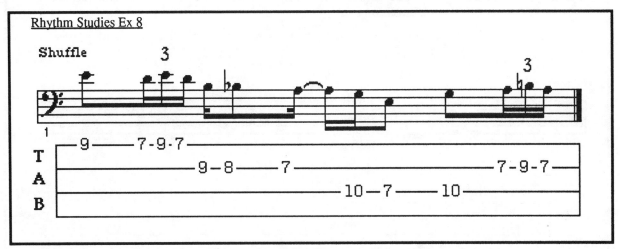

SIGHT READING ....

All of these rhythm studies have finally led us to the ultimate test in reading music: **sight reading**. Sight reading is reading and playing a piece of music you have never seen before from beginning to end without stopping. To be a good sight reader, you must have a very solid grasp of rhythm figures (like the ones we have been discussing), as well as a quick eye for reading notes on the staff.

Even the best sight readers will tell you that the only way to become and remain a good sight reader is to continually practice sight reading. Following are ten examples for you to sight read. Now, obviously you own this book and can therefore spend as much time as you want reviewing each piece until you have it memorized. That defeats the purpose, though.

I recommend that you **play through each exercise one time,** then move on to the next one. If you make a mistake, *keep going.* Play through all ten and then stop. Come back another day and play them again. I also suggest that you pick up other material to practice your sight reading. Any bass-clef music book will do, as will many piano books. Bach's *Two-Part Inventions* are always a fun challenge. Don't just look to bass books. Look to all sorts of other reading material. That is the best way to improve your sight-reading skills.

33

Sight Reading Ex 1

♩=104

Sight Reading Ex 2

♩=88

Sight Reading Ex 3

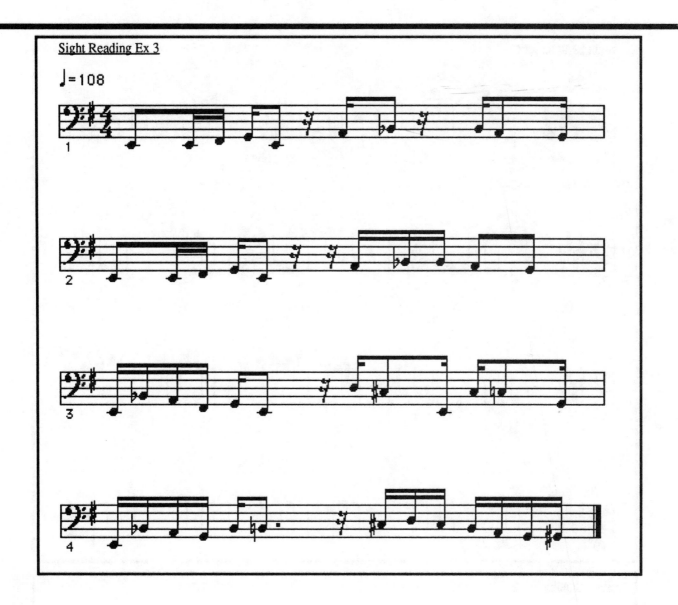

Sight Reading Ex 4

♩=144

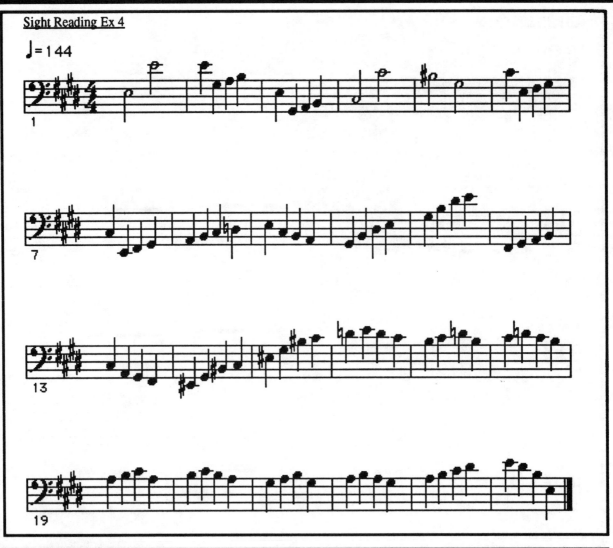

Sight Reading Ex 5

♩=138

Sight Reading Ex 6

Sight Reading Ex 7

Sight Reading Ex 8

♩=112

Sight Reading Ex 9

♩=126 (Shuffle)

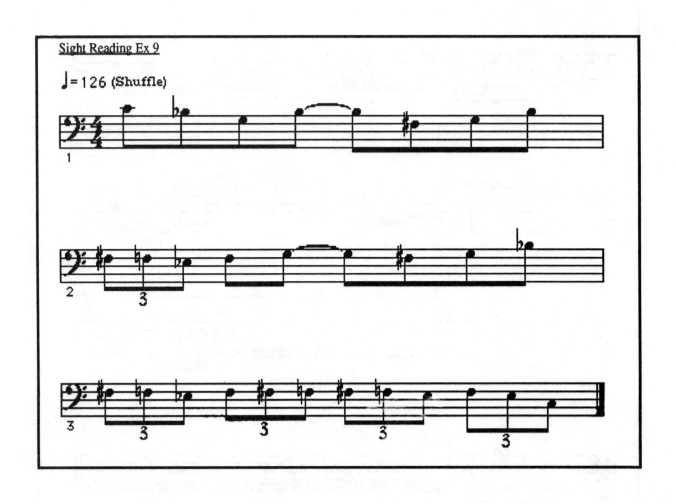

Sight Reading Ex 10

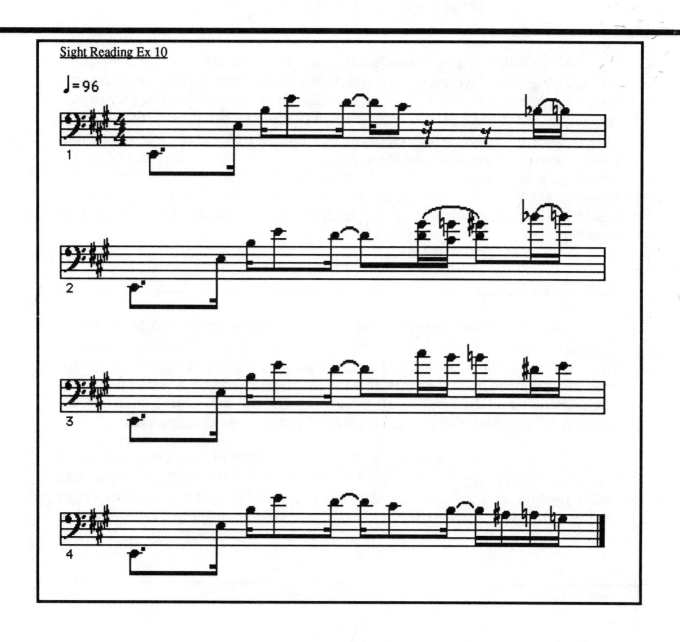

Playing Techniques

Many different playing techniques are incorporated into contemporary bass playing. These techniques are anything from minor inflections in the way a note is played to outright changes in right- and left-hand playing technique. It is important to have good control over all of these techniques so that you are always in control of your hand movements and the notes that you are playing. Poorly executed technique results in poorly executed notes. That means wrong notes, poor tone, bad timing; all the good qualities you want to have in your playing, right? No, of course not. So, let's talk about a few of them and play some bass lines that utilize these techniques in ways that you may use in your day-to-day playing.

TECHNIQUES ....

The first of these techniques we will look at is the **slide.** A slide is done by playing a note and then, without lifting the left-hand finger off of the note, *sliding* up or down to a different note. Slides can be played at different tempos. They also may be undefined as to the starting or ending point. That means you may start from any note and then end on a specific note. Or, you may start from a specific note and then slide off of it to an undefined note, or to no note at all.

Slides can be played with any finger of the left hand. Use a finger that sets up the note following the slide. That is, slide with the fourth finger if the note following the slide should be played with the first finger. That way, the first finger is already in position when the slide is complete. Here are a few examples of slides:

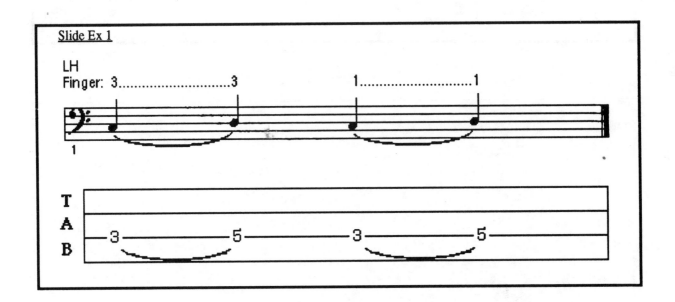

40

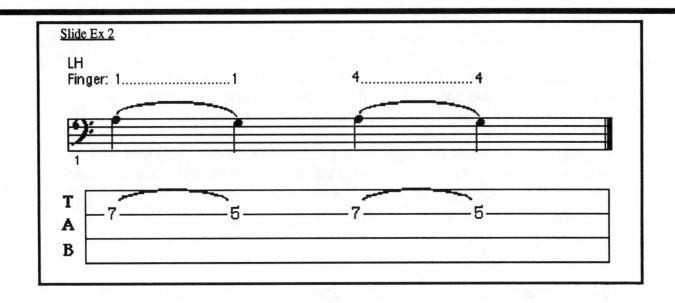

Slide Ex 2

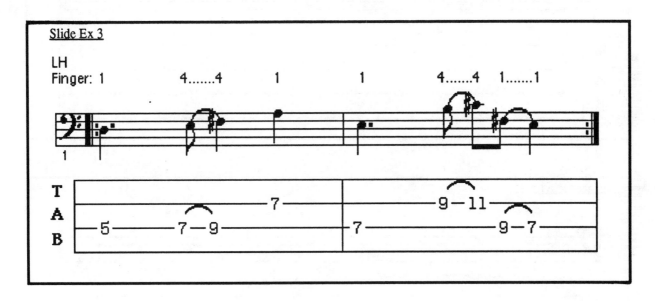

Slide Ex 3

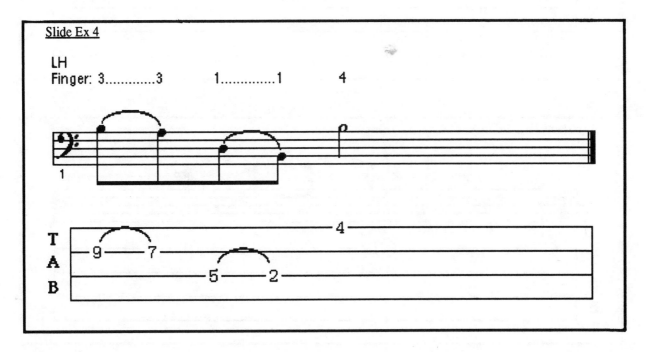

Slide Ex 4

A **grace note** is a note that is played very quickly and is barely audible relative to the note following it. Grace notes are written on the staff as the note that should be played; but the grace note is generally much smaller than the rest of the notes, and there is a diagonal line through its stem. There is also a tie between the grace note and the destination note, indicating it as a slide.

Grace notes may be played using any of the other techniques that are described in this section. As you learn each technique, try playing grace notes using that new technique. Here are a few examples:

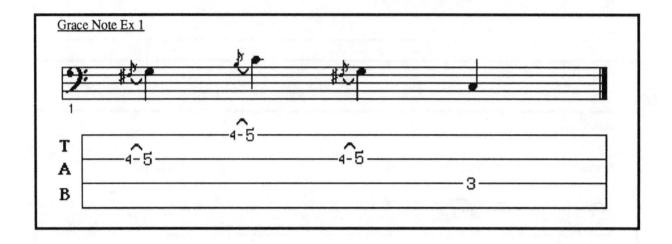

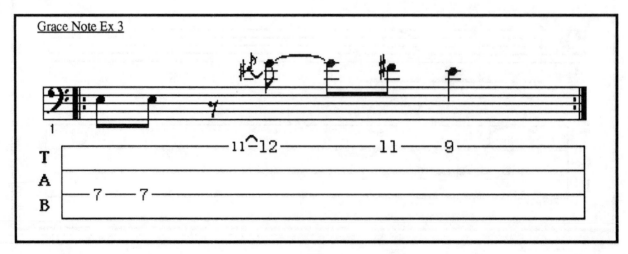

A **bend** is pretty self-explanatory. You grab a note and then bend it into another note. That pretty well covers it, huh? Notes may be bent up to another note, or even a semi-tone (not all the way to the next note). Also, you may bend the string before picking and then, without releasing the note, "unbend" the string back into the correct note for that fret. A bend can be written as a grace note or look like a slide (with a tie).

In the TAB diagrams below, the fret number in parentheses indicates the fret number to be *bent up to.* Thus, "(8)" means bend to the note at the 8th fret.

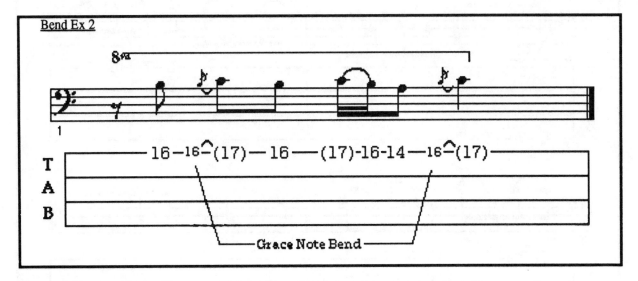

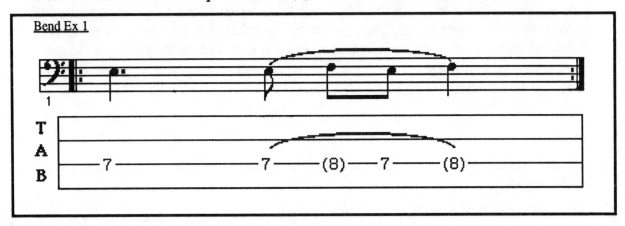

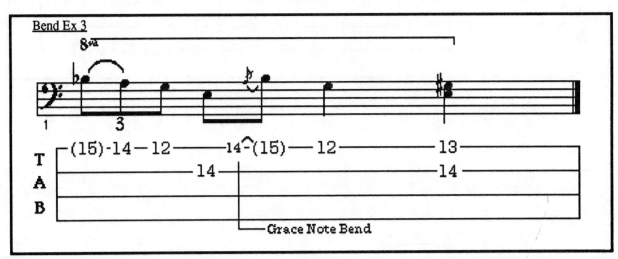

The **hammer-on** is a very important part of bass playing. This technique is played by picking the first note and then "hammering on" to the second note, without picking with the right hand. The second note is produced by the force of the left-hand finger pressing down that note. The interval between the two notes can realistically be any interval on the same string that your hand can stretch to. The following examples show whole-step, half-step, and extended-reach (minor third or 1½-step) intervals.

A couple of important facts about playing hammer-ons are that the first note is always lower in pitch than the second note and that only the first note is picked with the right hand. This technique produces a unique sound that is intended to be an alternative to picking both notes. I strongly urge you to fully master this technique, as it is very widely used and you will find it to be required in many situations.

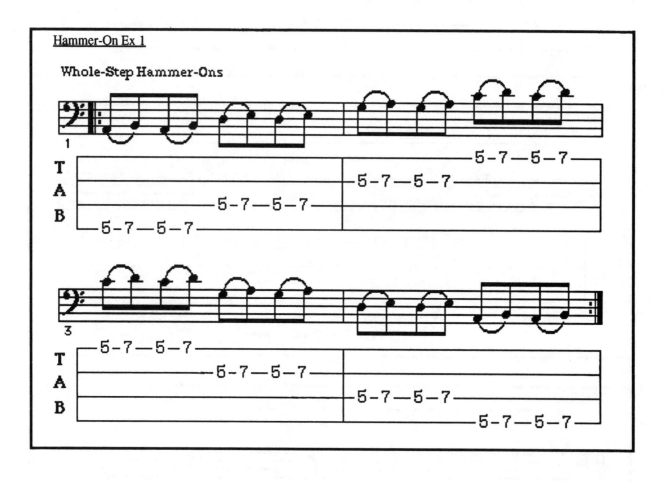

Hammer-On Ex 2

Half-Step Hammer-Ons

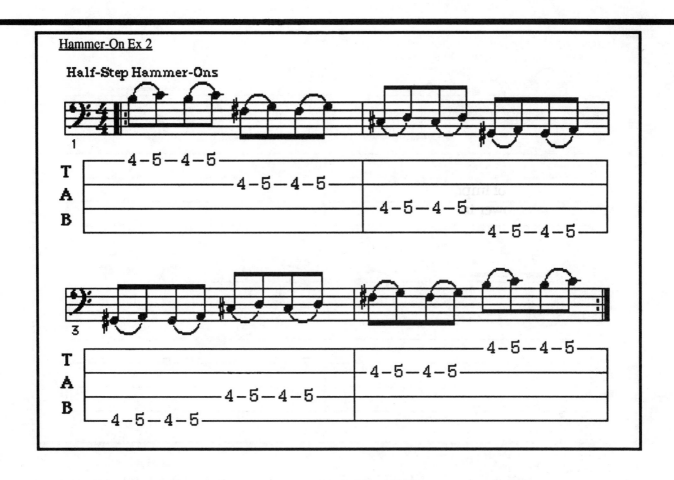

Hammer-On Ex 3

Extended-Reach (1-1/2 steps) Hammer-Ons

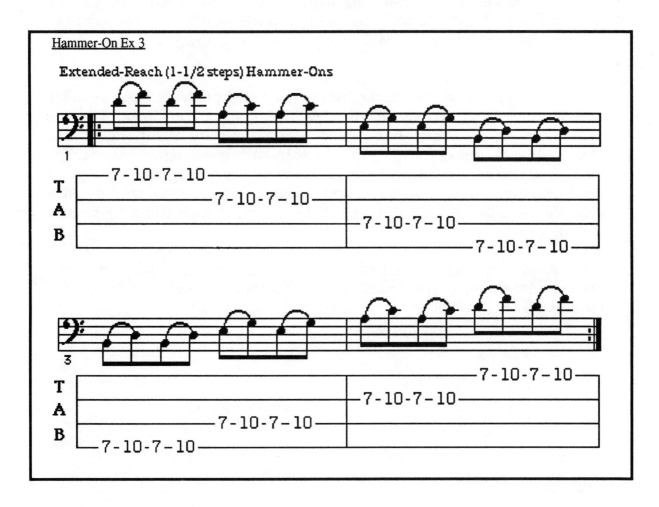

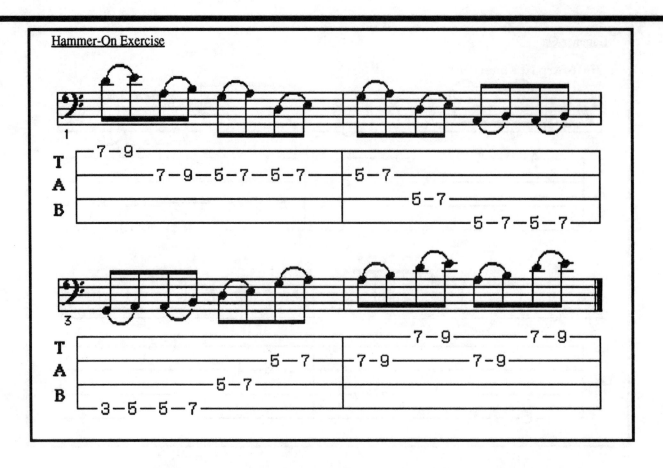

Hammer-On Exercise

The **pull-off** is the "sister" technique to the hammer-on because they really go hand in hand. Like the hammer-on, you only pick the first note of a pull-off. However, when playing a pull-off, the first note is always higher than the second note.

To play a pull-off, you actually fret two notes on the same string at the same time. For the sake of this explanation, fret the E-string at the 5th and 7th frets using the first and fourth left-hand fingers. Pick the first note with the right hand. Then, pull off the first note to the second note by slightly pulling the fourth finger towards the floor and off of the E-string. You should be pulling the E-string with the fourth finger so that the string springs back when released by the fourth finger, essentially "picking" the note at the 5th fret (which you have already fretted). Got it?

As with hammer-ons, pull-offs can be played at any interval you can reach. The following examples show whole-step, half-step, and extended-reach (minor third or 1½-step) pull-offs.

Pull-Off Ex 1

Whole-Step Pull-Offs

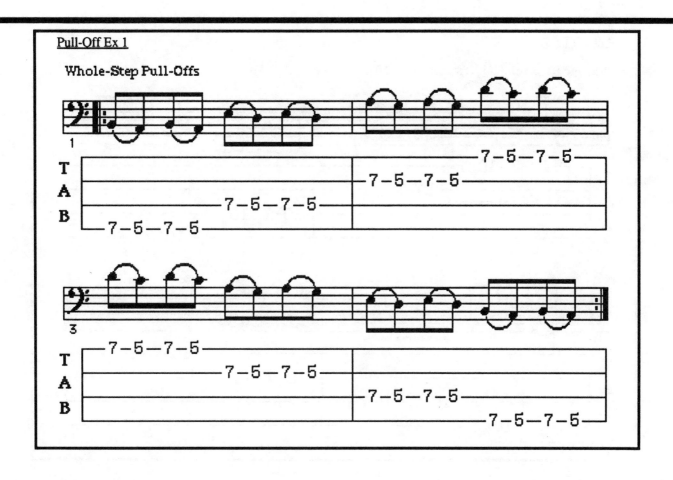

Pull-Off Ex 2

Half-Step Pull-Offs

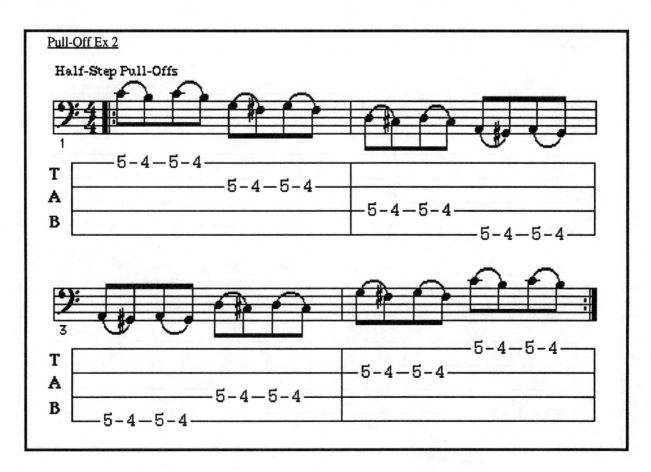

Pull-Off Ex 3

Extended Reach (1-1/2 steps) Pull-Offs

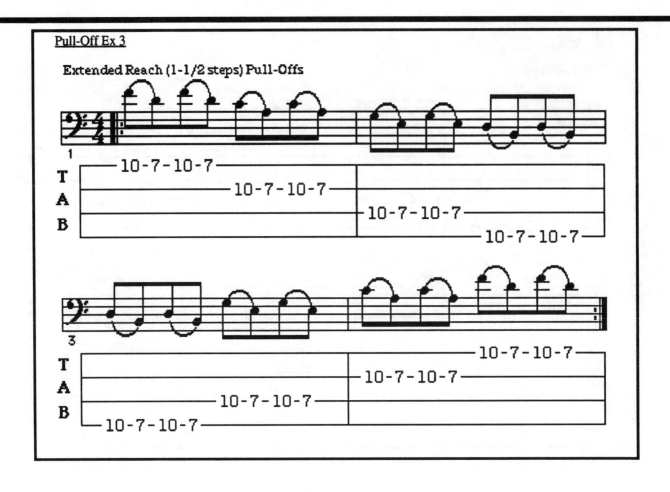

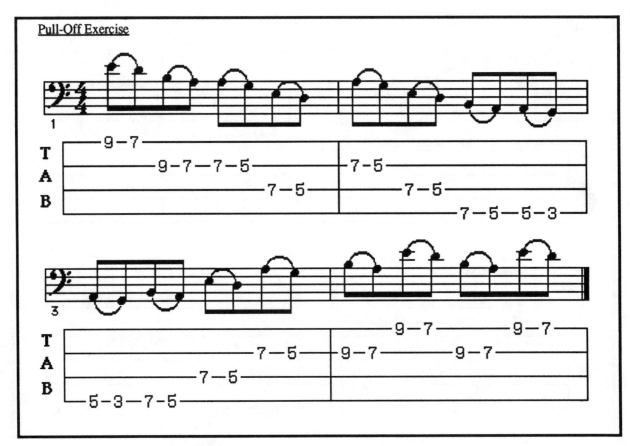

Here is an exercise that is made up of nothing but hammer-ons and pull-offs.

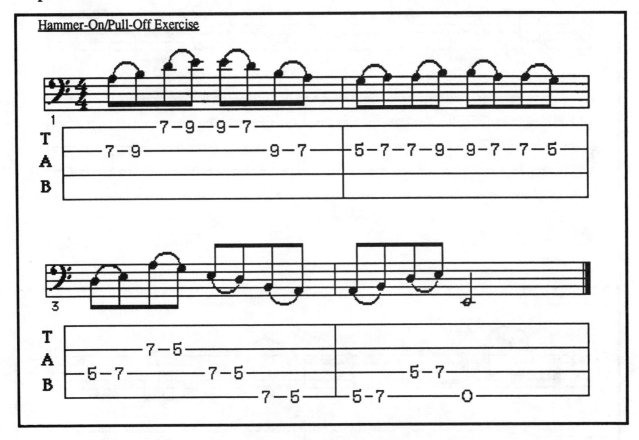

Hammer-On/Pull-Off Exercise

Playing a hammer-on immediately followed by a pull-off, without picking more than once, is called a **trill.** A trill consists of at least three notes—the first note, the second note, and then the first note again.

To play a trill, you simply pick the first note, hammer on to the second note, and then pull off back to the first note. Again, you *pick only the first note.*

Time-wise, a trill can be three notes (as in a sixteenth-note triplet, for example). Or, you may trill two notes for a specific length of time (i.e., two beats). To do this, you hammer on and pull off the two notes repeatedly as fast as you can. Trills can be a nice enhancement to a bass line or fill.

Trill Ex 1

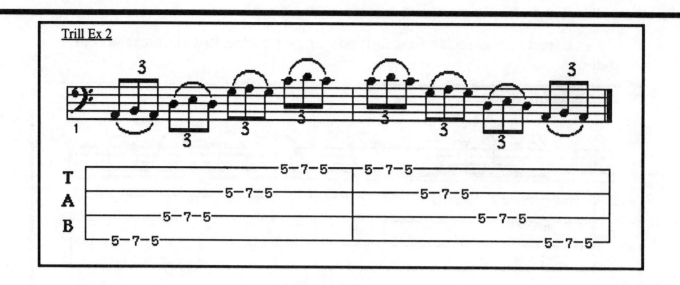

Trill Ex 2

Trill Ex 3

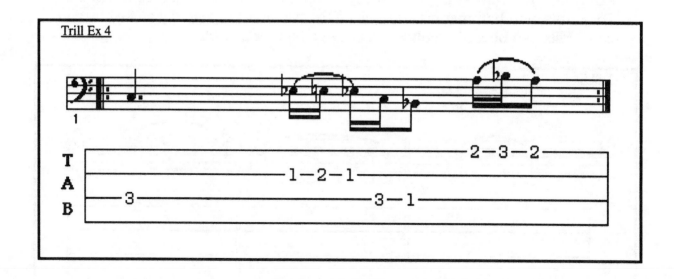

Trill Ex 4

50

Dead notes are probably my personal favorite when it comes to playing techniques. These little boogers can really make a bass line move! What is a dead note? A dead note is a note that is not really a note. (What?) It is a note that has *no tonal value*. It is strictly percussive in sound. A "click," if you will.

To play a dead note, lay the left-hand fingers across the strings without pressing down any notes. Now, pick a string with the right hand. Hear that click? That's the dead note. Incorporating these dead notes into a bass line requires some finesse. The following exercises will help you learn the technique.

NOTE: Dead notes are written as the letter "x" on the staff line or space of the open string on which they are to be played. An "x" on the staff space reserved for the open A-string means to pick the A-string while deadening the string with the left hand.

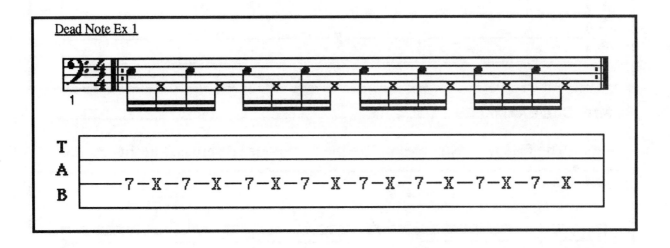

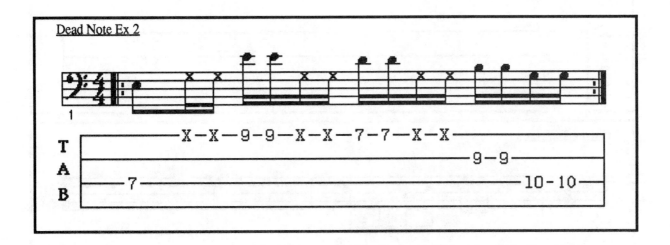

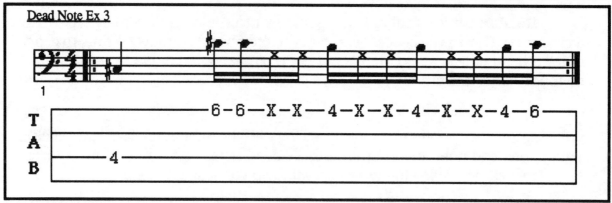

Dead Note Ex 3

```
T
A                 6-6—X—X—4—X—X—4—X—X—4—6
B       4
```

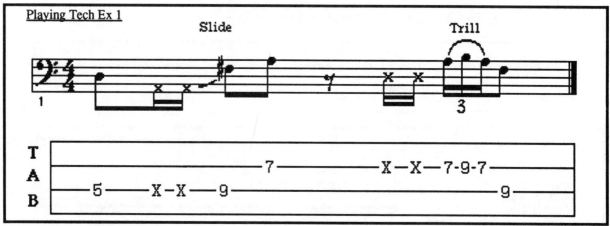

Dead Note Ex 4

```
T
A           X—4        X—5        X—6        7
B     5
```

MUSICAL EXAMPLES ....

The following examples utilize the techniques discussed in this section.

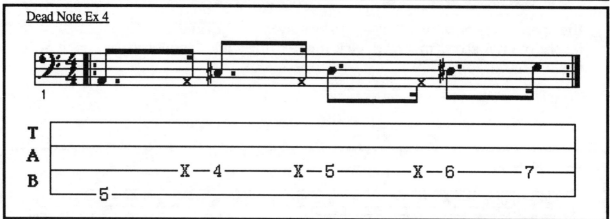

Playing Tech Ex 1

Slide   Trill

```
T
A                   7              X—X—7-9-7
B     5     X—X—9                              9
```

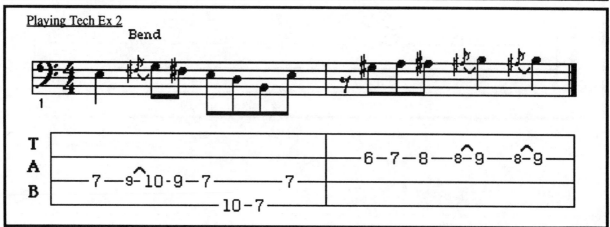

Playing Tech Ex 2

Bend

```
T
A                                   6—7—8—8⌣9—8⌣9
B     7—9⌣10-9-7        7
              10-7
```

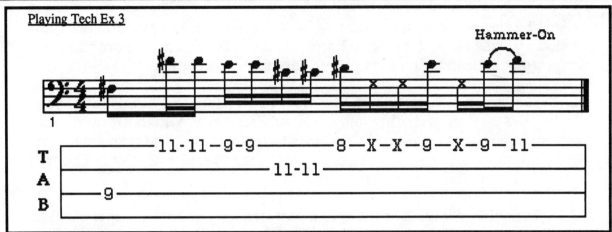

Playing Tech Ex 3

Hammer-On

```
      11-11-9-9          8-X-X-9-X-9-11
T                11-11
A
B  9
```

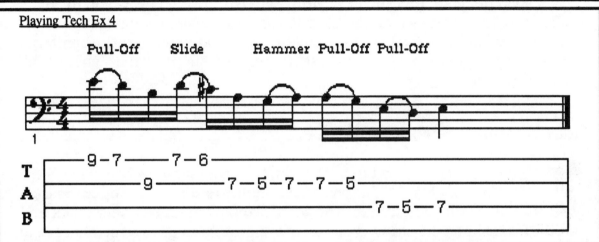

Playing Tech Ex 4

Pull-Off Slide   Hammer Pull-Off Pull-Off

```
    9-7      7-6
T        9       7-5-7-7-5
A
B                    7-5-7
```

Playing Tech Ex 5

Pull-Off   Pull-Off   Pull-Off   Pull-Off

```
    5-4      5-4       5-4       5-4       5-6-7
T        7        7         7         7
A
B
```

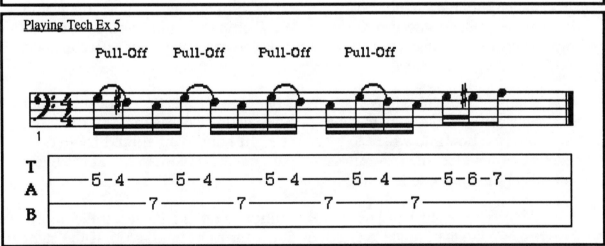

Playing Tech Ex 6

Trill

```
T                                    5-6-5-6
                               5-7
A
B  5-X-6-7-5    3    4    5-X-6-7-5
```

53

Slap and Pop

The **slap-and-pop** technique is one of the most popular techniques used in modern bass playing. You can hardly listen to the radio for more than two songs without hearing the bass player slap or pop something!

Slap and pop is also one of the most challenging and fun techniques to master. It is a study of rhythm more than anything else. Variations on rhythm patterns are a very key element in slap. Many times you'll be groovin' on one rhythm pattern and then vary it from time to time to create breaks or changes in the rhythms. This can be very exciting!

To do this, a large "library" of different rhythm patterns is required. Also, a very solid understanding of the rhythm patterns involved helps you to create different patterns and variations on patterns you are already familiar with. As time goes on, you will find that you are able to ad-lib and create parts and patterns at will, without thinking about it, just "feeling" it. And isn't that what it's all about anyway?

RIGHT-HAND TECHNIQUE ....

The right hand is the key to the slap technique, mainly because it's the hand that does the slappin'! The basic technique is to slap the string *against the fretboard* using the right thumb. The act of slapping must be a very quick and accurate attack on the string. A couple of important things to remember are to always keep your right hand and forearm relaxed so it's easier to move freely, and that there's really no need to do your "Mr. T" impersonation and break your thumb because you slap the string too hard! You can't play slap with a cast on your hand, so take it easy!

Hand placement is important. Your right hand must be in a position that is relaxed, comfortable, easy to move, and free to do all of the things it must do. I will describe how and where to place the right hand. You should try to do it exactly as I describe; then, over time, you can make adjustments that will allow you to feel the most comfortable.

Place your right hand so that the right thumb is almost parallel to the fourth string (a slight angle is OK). Position your right hand so that the right thumb is just over the last fret or so of the fretboard. At this time the right-hand fingers should be lying flat across the strings. The bottom "fleshy" part of your right hand (called the "heel") should be touching the fourth string. Let's talk about what role each of the three parts of your right hand will play when you slap:

> **The THUMB:** The thumb is used to slap the strings. You will need to learn to slap all four of the strings (individually). To slap a note, quickly slap the string against the fretboard with the thumb. The thumb should "bounce" back off of the string very quickly, so as not to kill or mute the note when it is slapped.

The HEEL: The heel is used to mute, or deaden, selected notes. One common use will be to keep lower strings from ringing when you are playing on the first, second, or third strings. Developing control over the use of the heel of the right hand is very tricky and just as important.

The FINGERS: The first and second fingers are used to "pop" notes on the first, second, and sometimes third strings. Popping is done by curving the fingertip under the string and pulling the string away from the fretboard, then releasing the string so that the string slaps back against the fretboard. Be very careful not to grab the string with too much of the finger, as you may pull the string right off of the bass! Use the first finger to pop notes on the second and third strings, and use the second finger to pop notes on the first string.

The act of slapping and popping should be a "down-up" technique. Follow me as I explain what I mean by "down-up":

1) In order to slap or pop any note, the hand must first be raised away from the strings.

2) To slap a note, the entire right hand is brought *down*, allowing the thumb to slap the note against the fretboard as described above. This is the **"down"** stroke.

3) Once again, to slap or pop another note, the hand must be raised away from the strings. As the hand is being raised, popped notes are played with the first or second finger. This is the **"up"** stroke. If the next note is supposed to be slapped instead of popped, you would raise the hand and then slap the second note.

Popped notes are played on the **"up"** stoke *after* a slapped note.

There is a natural tendency to play the slap/pop technique using a rotation, or alternating, method by which the hand is rotated at the wrist and notes are basically alternated slap, pop, slap, pop. I have found that the "down-up" technique will allow you to play much faster. This is because the pop is done on an "up" stroke, so there is no energy exerted to play that note. It is a natural movement as a result of the slap. Obviously, in some rhythm patterns, popped notes do not always follow slapped notes. In these instances you must improvise on the "down-up" method to achieve the desired pattern.

Another problem with rotating the hand at the wrist is that the thumb is allowed to come away from the fretboard as much as 3"-4"!! No, no, no, no, no!! Why would you want your poor wrist to have to do so much work to get your thumb back on the same planet as the string it must slap in the next fraction of a second?!? I guess if you wanted sloppy technique and very little control over your hands, then you could let your thumb fly all over the place......but I wouldn't recommend it!

LEFT-HAND TECHNIQUE ....

The left hand provides the "finesse" in slap playing. With the left hand you will hold, choke, add vibrato, bend, trill, slide, hammer, (and on and on...) the notes that your right hand is dishing out. If you are playing open strings, the left hand is used to cut off, or choke, the notes to provide a more staccato feel. In the exercises to follow, you should try each experiment using different feels with the left hand. Try 'em with vibrato or without vibrato. Cut the notes short, or let them ring long. Try different approaches to establish your own "library" of techniques and feels with the left hand. In the exercises that follow, I will make suggestions on left-hand exercises as well as techniques.

OK, let's play some. We'll start out simple to establish the proper technique. Then we will learn some different rhythm patterns. After that, we will learn how to create variations on given rhythm patterns. Have a good time with this stuff—it's really fun!!

EXERCISES ....

As I mentioned before, slap playing is a serious study in rhythm. In the exercises that follow, we will experiment with different variations on each type of note (quarter, eighth, and sixteenth). Each rhythm pattern is two bars long. Repeat that rhythm pattern until you feel as though you are in the groove of the pattern. Then proceed. Be sure that you can play all the way through all of the quarter-note rhythm patterns at the same tempo, without stopping, before you move to the eighth-note patterns. It is very important that you be able to smoothly change between rhythm patterns without breaking the groove. At the end, I have mixed up the quarter-note rhythm patterns with eighth-note rhythms for you to test your "interchangeability." (Nice guy, huh?)

I also strongly recommend that you practice with a metronome or a drum machine when doing these exercises. That will really help you develop a good sense of time and rhythm. You can even program the drum machine to play the exact rhythm pattern you are working on. Then you have a steady reference of what the pattern should sound like.

One more piece of advice, then I'll shut up and let you play.............. **GO SLOWLY!!!** My dad once gave me a good piece of advice when he said, "Slow down and you'll go faster!" It is very important to go slowly and make sure you get the basics of the technique down cold. If your foundation is weak, your playing will have poor timing, control, and feel. Speed comes with time. Allow yourself that time and you'll be much better off.

To start, play the following quarter-note rhythm patterns using the "slap" method described above. These exercises use only the right-hand thumb—there is no "popping" yet. Play them slowly until you develop a consistent feel from one pattern to the next. Each note should be strong, solid, and well defined. Use the left hand to let the notes ring as true quarter notes, the full length of the beat.

Note that this exercise is written with *all notes being the open E-string.* After you feel comfortable with the rhythm patterns, try the same rhythms using the G and then the A notes on the 3rd and 5th frets of the E-string to get used to the left-hand technique when slapping.

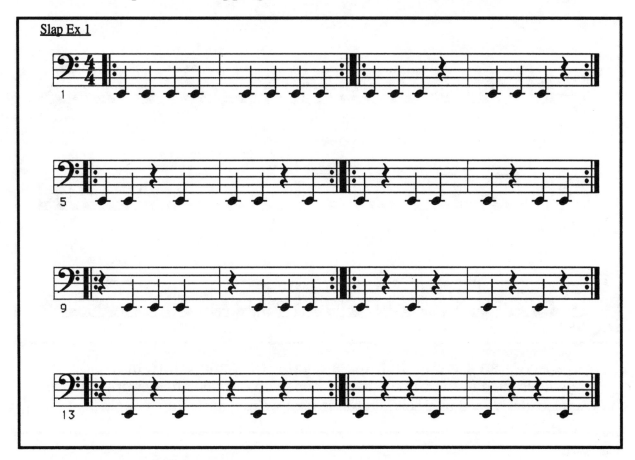

OK, here comes the eighth-note study. Do this one the same as the quarter-note study above, except this time use the left hand to let the notes ring long or to cut off or choke the notes for a more staccato feel. So, first learn the rhythm patterns, letting the notes ring for their full value. Then, go back and try to change to a more staccato feel by choking the notes with the left hand. (Choking is done by lifting the left hand off of the fretboard, without letting the string ring freely. It is advisable to allow all four fingers of the left hand to touch the string to stop it from vibrating, thus "choking" it.) *This exercise is written on the open A-string.* Try it using the G (E-string), C (A-string), and any other notes on either the A- or E-strings.

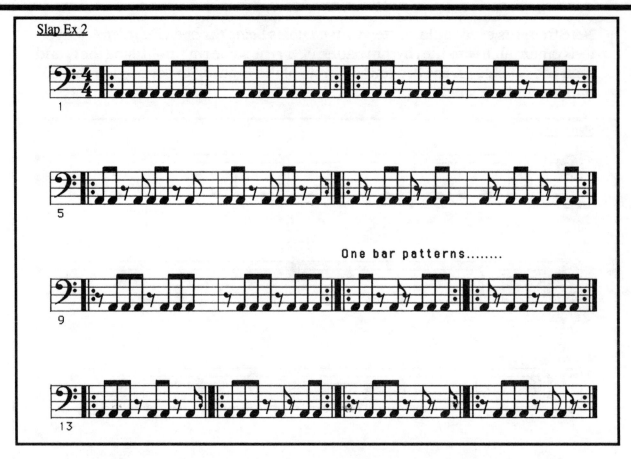

Here's an exercise that mixes quarter-note and eighth-note patterns, sometimes even in the same bar, so I hope you did your homework! Get this exercise down good and solid, because next we're gonna start poppin'!!

As mentioned before, "popping" is done using the right-hand first finger to pop the second string and the right-hand second finger to pop the first string. Let's get you used to the idea and feel of popping notes before we start combining slapping and popping. This is where the left-hand technique really comes into play. A "popped" note does not sustain very long. And, if you let it ring, it's usually not a very attractive sound. So most of the time you must "choke" or cut off the note, making it pretty short. The more you pop notes, the better you will be at working the left hand to really get the most tone out of the notes.

For the following exercises, you need to concentrate on getting a good, solid, and clear tone out of each note. Also, you need to get the first and second fingers on your right hand used to the feel of popping so they always grab just enough of the string to get a good "pop" without getting your hand "caught up" under the string.

So, here's an exercise that is ALL POPPING. Do not slap any of these notes. Remember to pop the notes on the G-string with the second finger, and the notes on the D-string with the first finger. Check the tablature below to see where to play each note.

59

OK, now let's try alternating slaps and pops. Without a doubt, the most common pattern for the slap technique is the octave pattern. It is done simply by alternating between a note and the next higher octave of that same note.

The next pattern is an example of a quarter-note octave pattern. Remember that, when you alternate slapping and popping, you should use the "down-up" technique that I described earlier. The goal is a smooth, easy rhythm of down-up-down-up.

Now, here is an eighth-note octave pattern to work with. Use both this eighth-note pattern and the above quarter-note pattern to really get familiar with the feel of slapping and popping.

Here are a couple of octave-pattern technique exercises to really get you used to slapping and popping. Use these as warm-up exercises before you start playing.

It is very important that you do some warm-up exercises before you start slapping/popping. This technique is very physical and it is not uncommon to get cramps in your hands and forearms if you do not properly warm up!

The following exercises will help you get properly warmed up. Play them *slowly* at first, then build up some speed.

Slap Ex 7

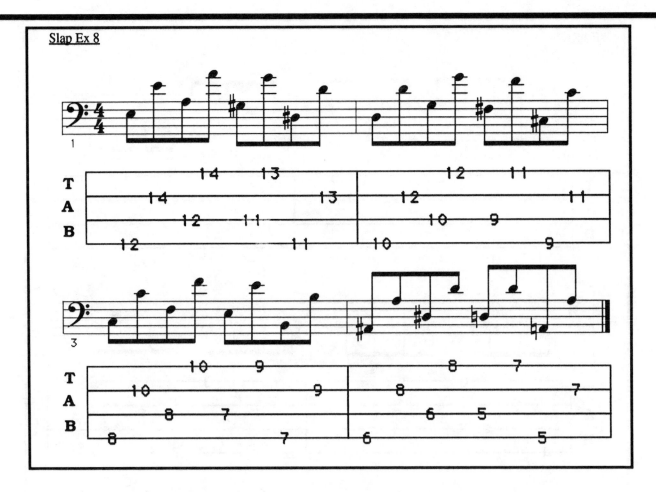

Slap Ex 8

RHYTHM PATTERNS ....

We are going to stick with the octave patterns while learning some different rhythm patterns (because they are simple to play!). However, feel free to play around with any other intervals you want. That's where the best ideas for new bass lines come from anyway!

Here are a few simple rhythm patterns to get you used to playing some different combinations of slap/pop alternations. Use the tablature to see where to play the notes. Again, experiment with different left-hand techniques to allow the notes to sustain or be choked.

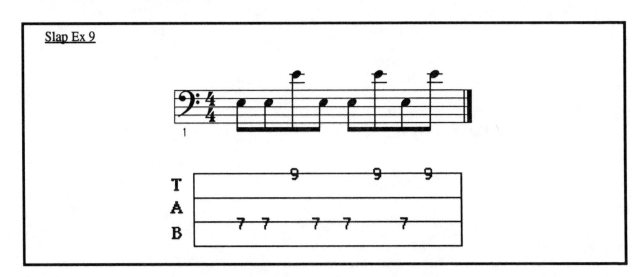

Slap Ex 9

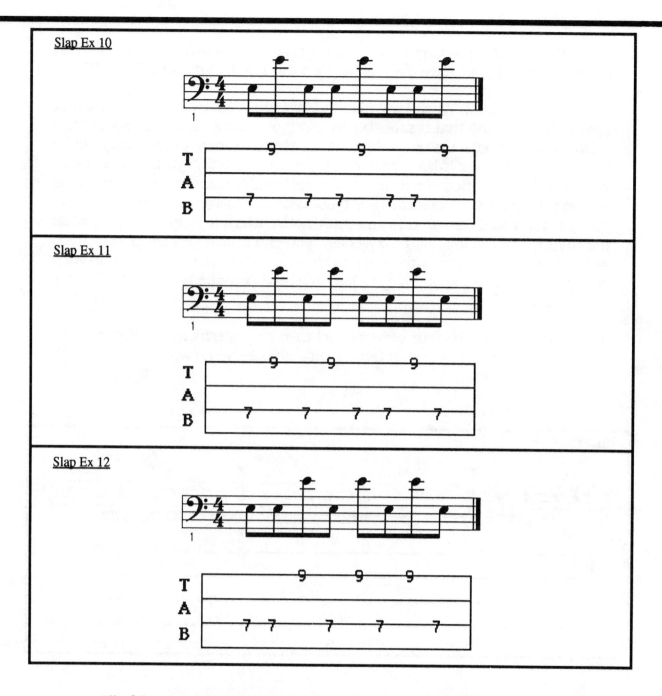

All of the previous exercises were eighth-note patterns. If we take the first one and re-write it as a sixteenth-note pattern, here's what we get:

We have taken a simple eighth-note pattern and re-written it as sixteenth notes. Essentially, we have made a simple pattern a little more difficult. Right?

Well, sort of..... When I say "difficult," we are probably both thinking that I mean "faster." And that is probably true in most cases. However, "speed" is a result of the tempo. If the tempo is slow, the sixteenth-note pattern may not be fast at all! The concept to learn here is this: You can convert rhythm patterns into whatever denomination of note (quarter note, eighth note, sixteenth note) is the easiest to help you understand it! So, if you come across a difficult sixteenth-note pattern, you could convert it to an eighth-note pattern to help determine what the rhythm sounds like. And, conversely, you can take an eighth-note pattern and convert it into a sixteenth-note pattern to see what it's like in a certain song or bass line. This is the first step in learning how to create your own variations on rhythm patterns.

Let's convert the four previous eighth-note patterns into sixteenth-note patterns. Play them so you can feel the difference between where the notes fall relative to each beat.

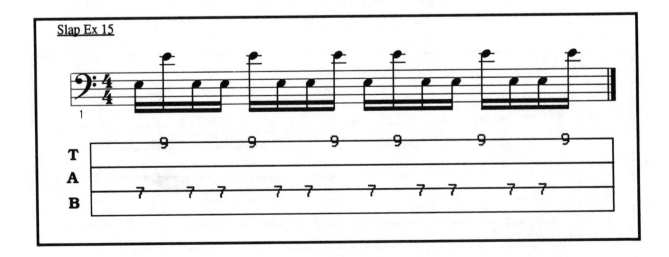

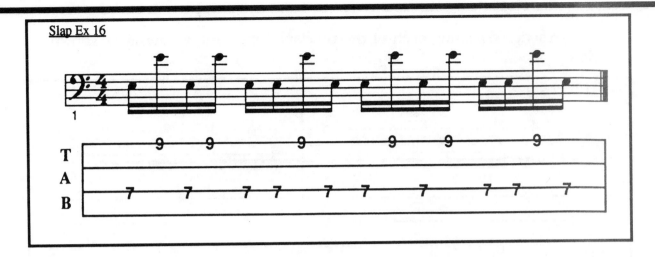

Slap Ex 16

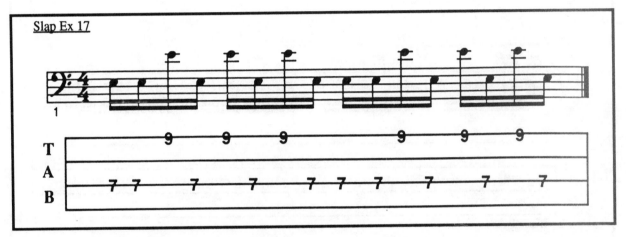

Slap Ex 17

The previous four exercises are variations on a rhythm pattern that is four beats long. Let's create some variations on just one beat of the pattern.

As you can see, the pattern consists of three "slapped" lower octaves and one "popped" upper octave with the difference between each beat being the placement of the "popped" upper octave. In any one beat, there are four possible places for the "pop" to occur; on the first, second, third, or fourth sixteenth note of the beat:

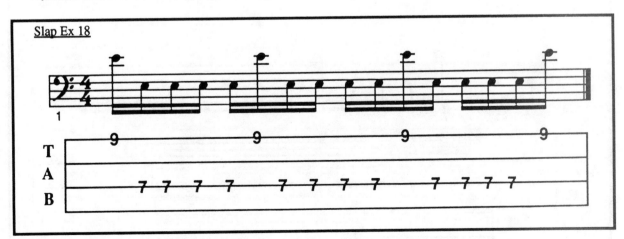

Slap Ex 18

Practice repeating each of the previous "one-beat" patterns as shown below:

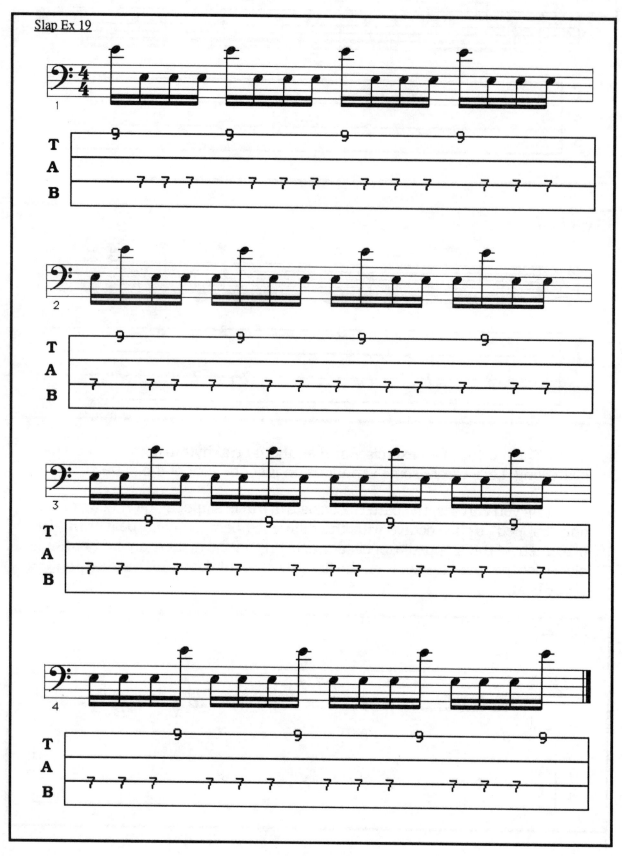

Next, we need to be able to alternate between any of these four "one-beat" rhythm patterns in any order. Here's a couple of examples. You should work out some of your own exercises to further your understanding of this concept. (Sometimes just reading out of a book doesn't cut it! A little experimentation can go a long way!)

Here are some rhythm patterns to work with. I'm just throwing in some eighth- and sixteenth-note combinations to give you some other ideas. Work with these rhythm patterns the same as we did the straight sixteenth-note patterns. Make as many variations as you can. Also, notice the letters above the music. Now that we're going to be mixing up different notes and rhythm patterns, I will start identifying which notes are slapped (T = Thumb) and popped (P = Popped).

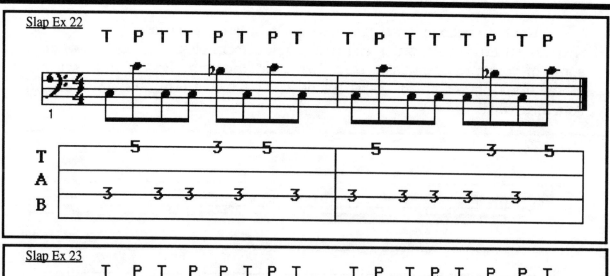

Slap Ex 22

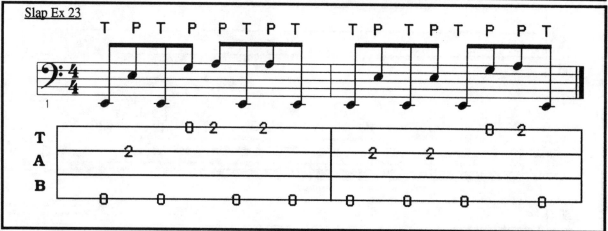

Slap Ex 23

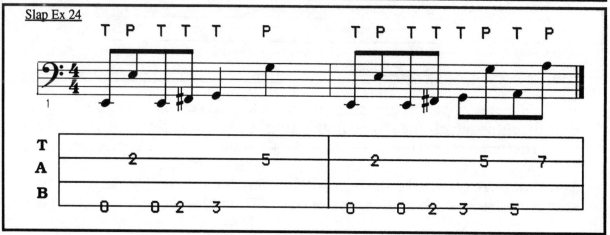

Slap Ex 24

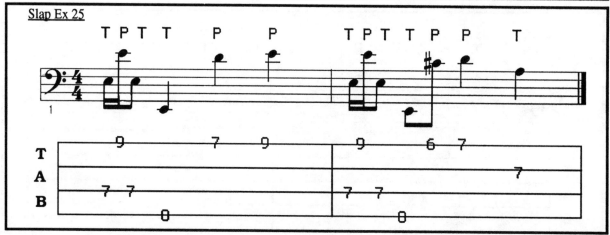

Slap Ex 25

68

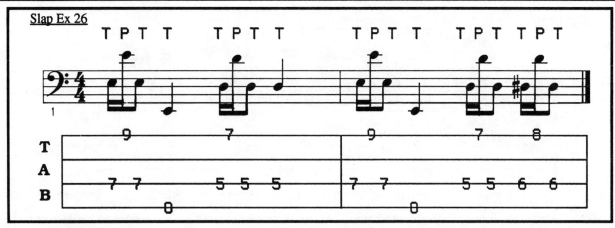

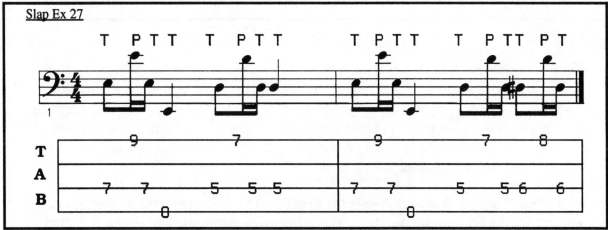

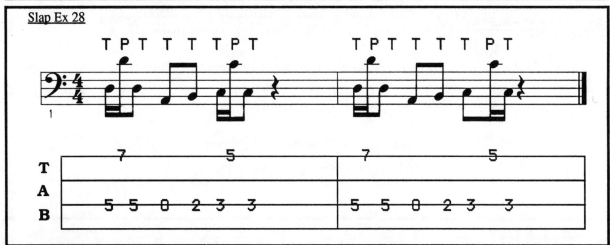

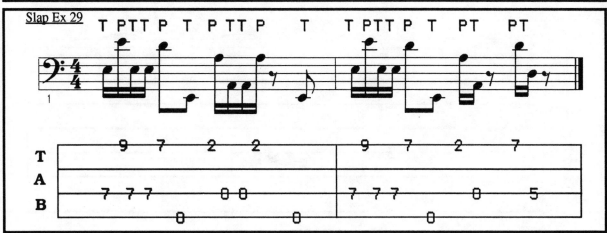

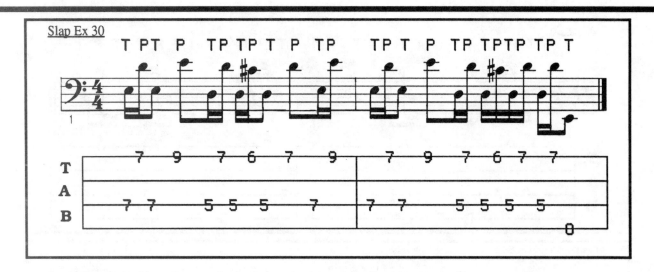

SLAP-AND-POP TECHNIQUES ....

Hammer-ons and pull-offs are two of the most important parts of the slap-and-pop technique, with the exception of the actual slapping and popping! Previously discussed in the "Playing Techniques" section of this book, you should already be familiar with how to play hammer-ons and pull-offs. They are a part of day-to-day bass playing for most players.

Hammer-ons and pull-offs are techniques that are used by the left hand to create different effects. In slap-and-pop playing, while the left hand is hammering on and pulling off, the right hand may be slapping or popping; it works both ways. Let's take a look at hammer-ons and pull-offs.......

Before we get too far, for those who don't know what a hammer-on is, refer back to the previous section on playing techniques for an explanation of how to play hammer-ons.

In the exercise below, you will be slapping on each beat and hammering to the eighth note between the beats.

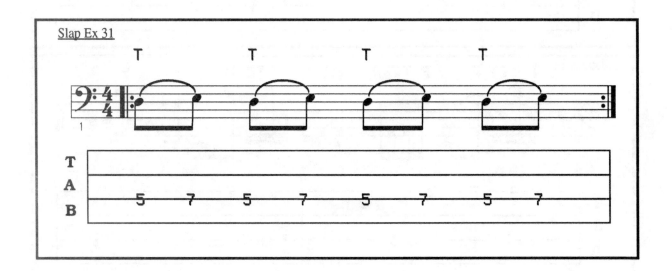

In this exercise, you will be popping on each beat and hammering to the eighth note between the beats.

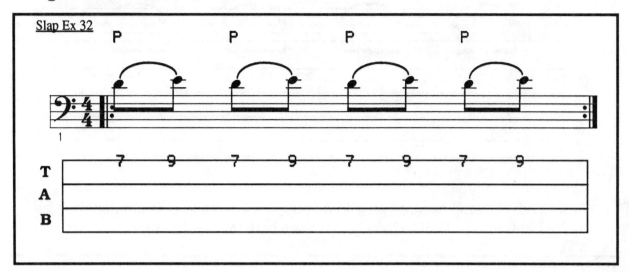

Here's an exercise that alternates between slapping and popping hammer-ons. Again, you are slapping/popping on the beat and hammering to the eighth note between the beats.

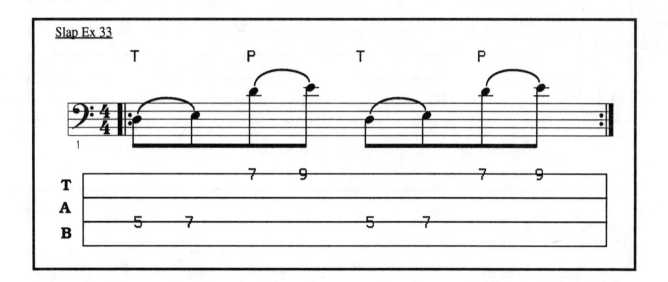

The pull-off is the "sister" technique to the hammer-on, also explained in the previous section on playing techniques. Look for the explanation of how to play pull-offs there.

The following exercise should be slapped. (And we know how painful that can be!) Sorry. Slap each of the notes that fall on the beat, and pull off to the eighth notes between the beats.

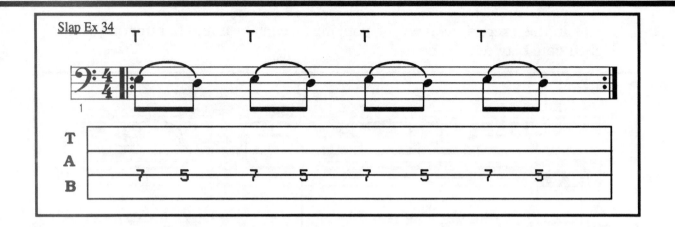

The following exercise should be popped. Pop each of the notes that fall on the beat, and pull off to the eighth notes between the beats.

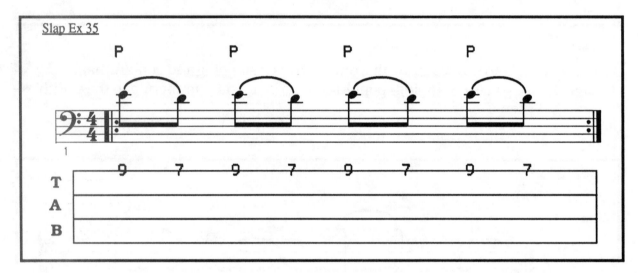

Here's one that alternates slapping and popping using pull-offs:

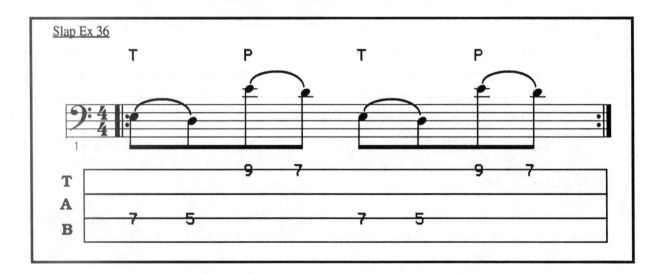

OK, let's try alternating hammer-ons and pull-offs while slapping and popping, all wrapped up into one exercise:

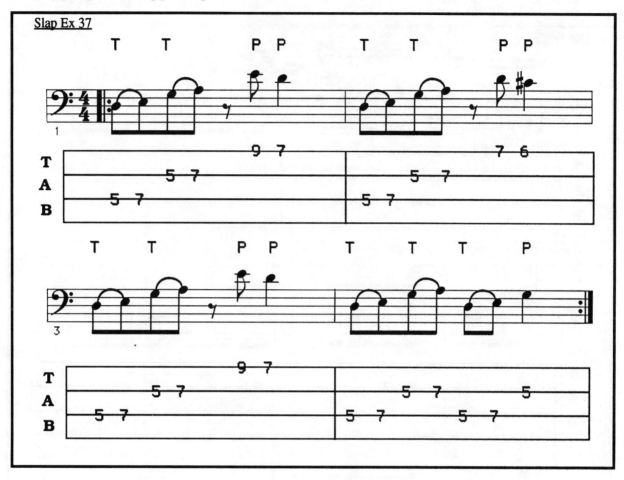

73

Here are a couple of exercises that should be practiced to develop solid, smooth, and consistent hammer-ons and pull-offs.

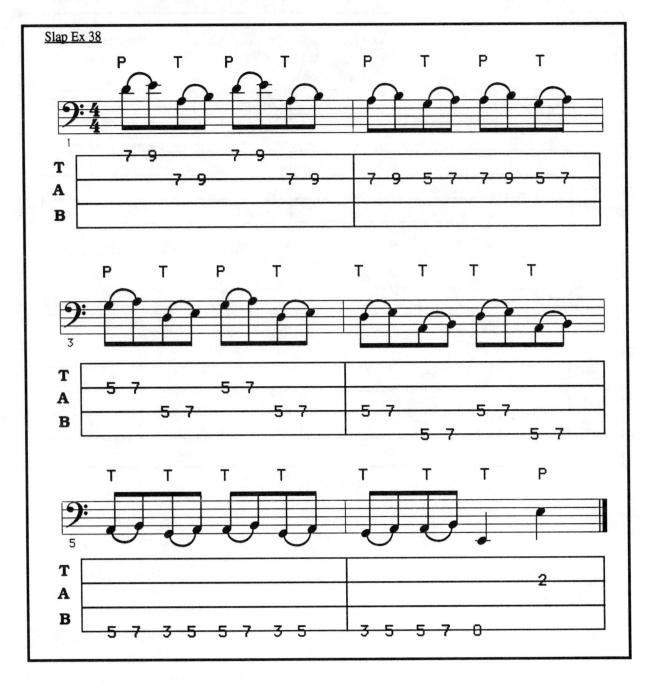

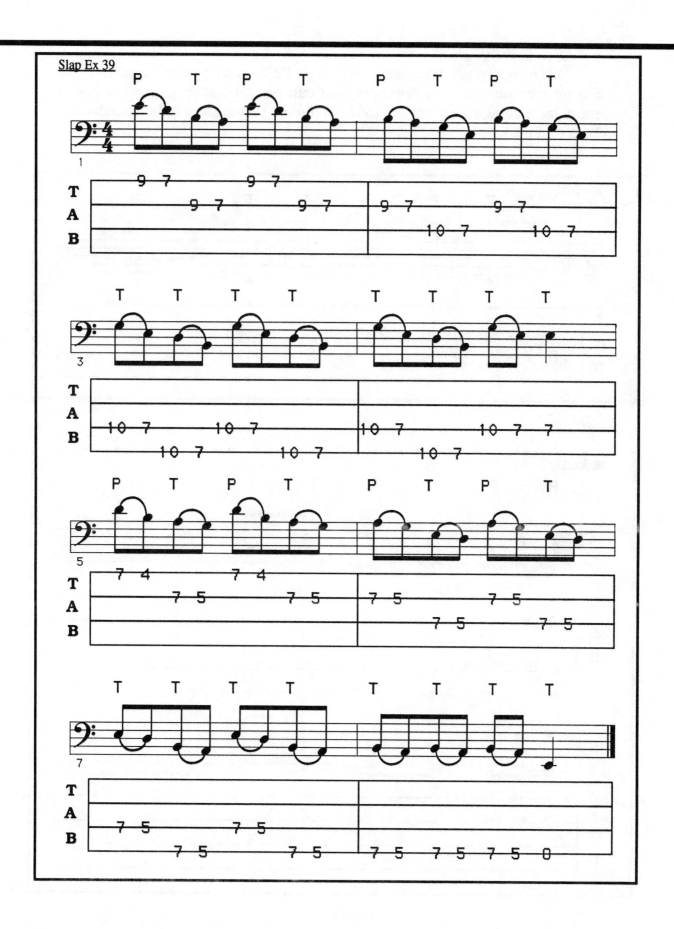

OK, now let's use hammer-ons and pull-offs in some slap patterns. One thing to remember is this: Any note that can be slapped or popped is also a candidate for being a hammer-on and/or a pull-off (as long as it fits rhythmically). Let's try some.....

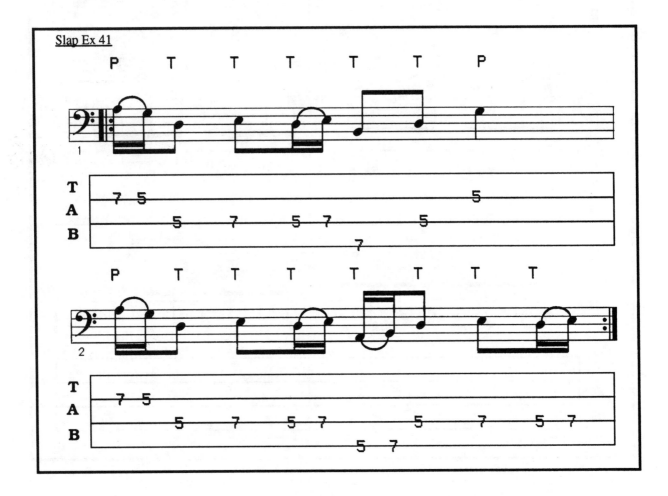

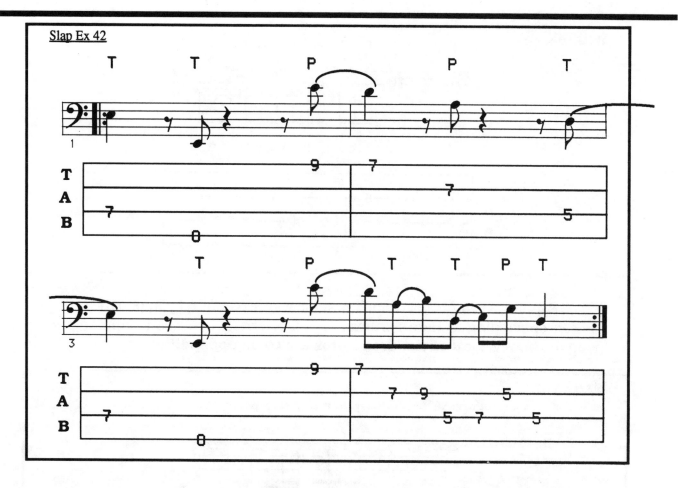

Slap Ex 42

Well, there is one more aspect of slap playing that we must discuss before I turn you loose on the world to *"do that voodoo that you do"*!! It's a technique called **dead notes.** Once again, to those of you who have listened to Tower of Power, dead notes are a part of many players' day-to-day technical skills. (See the previous section on playing techniques for an explanation of "dead notes.") They can be played in normal playing styles by choking, or muting, the string and then picking it. This produces a "click" or "thud" type of a sound.

In slap-and-pop playing, dead notes are used to achieve a more percussive effect than a musical one. And, when you're groovin' on a funk pattern, there ain't nothin' gonna make the line move more than a few well-placed dead notes!!

Dead notes can be played three ways: slapping with the right hand, popping with the right hand, and slapping with the left hand. That's right, I said slapping with the left hand! Let's look at the other two ways first.

To slap a dead note, simply lay your left hand across the strings, preferably with all four fingers touching the strings. Being careful not to fret a note, slap a string with the right hand. You should hear a "thud" or dead sound—not a note. If you hear a note, then you are not muting the strings correctly with the left hand.

Believe it or not, I have an exercise for this!! (Am I prepared, or what?!?) In the music that follows, the "x" signifies the dead note. The line or space that the "x" is on signifies which string to slap with the right hand. Try it.....

77

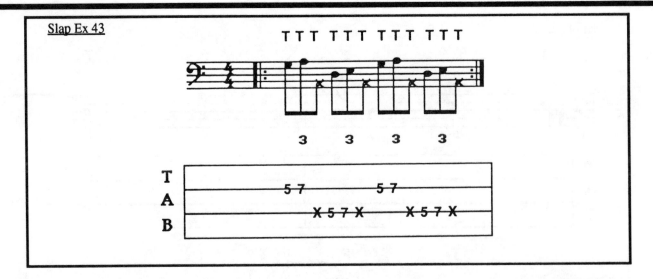

Popping a dead note is done the same way, except that you pop the string instead of slapping it. Here's an example. It alternates between slapping and popping; however, **all of the dead notes are to be popped!!**

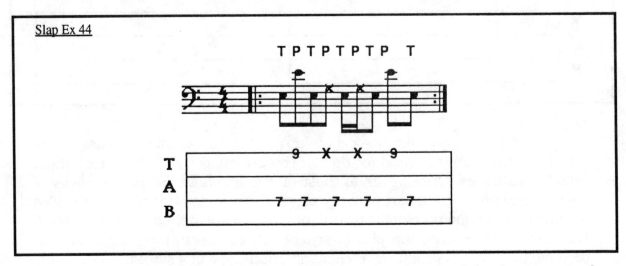

Now for a combination exercise of slapped and popped dead notes mixed in with real notes.

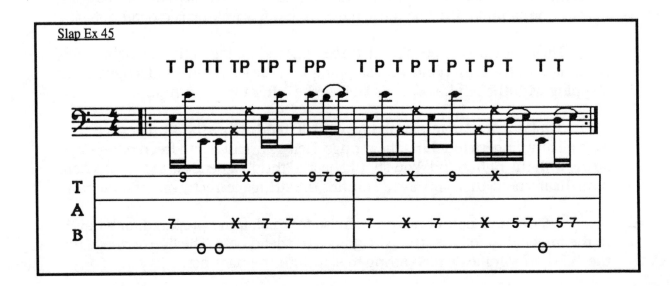

Most of the dead notes you will find yourself playing will probably be slapped. So, here is an exercise that will help you with it rhythmically. Practice repeating the exercise to get your feel for dead notes to be as smooth and consistent as all the other notes you play.

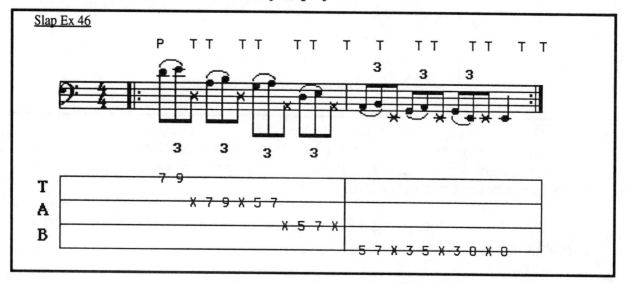

Playing dead notes with the left hand is one of the more advanced techniques in slap-style playing. It requires a serious amount of control over the left hand. This is because, in addition to having your right hand flopping all over the place, slapping and popping like crazy, your left hand is also going nuts trying to fret notes as well as play dead notes. Sound a little wild? It sure is....

Try this.... Imitate a drummer by slapping the strings with your right hand, then your left hand. Don't let the strings ring. There should only be dead notes. Alternate right-left-right-left, etc....

That is similar to the effect we will be shooting for. The left-hand slap is not played very hard. In fact, all it does is make the strings touch the frets, creating the dead-note sound. It may not seem loud, but that is not so important. The important thing is the feel that it creates, similar to a drum or percussion part.

Do this.... Slap the open E-string with your right hand. Next, slap the strings with the left hand, creating a dead note. You may need to mute some strings with your right hand.

Now play this: E, left-hand dead note, followed by another open E. Let's try repeating that sequence in rhythm, like this:

(**NOTE:** From here on, the "L" in the tablature indicates a left-hand dead note.)

Slap Ex 47

Again, the technique is similar to playing drums on the edge of a table, alternating right, left, right, left..... Be sure to repeat the above exercise enough times to really get the hang of it.

Now, let's try doing a right-hand slap, a left-hand dead note, and then a popped note. Like this:

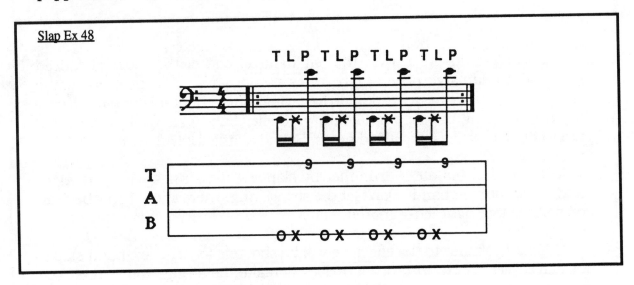

Slap Ex 48

Another rhythm for this might be eighth-note triplets:

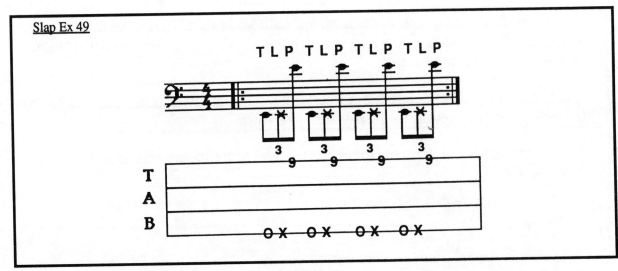

Slap Ex 49

Here's yet another rhythm. This time there is a left-hand dead note, followed by a right-hand dead note (slapped), followed by a popped note. Play this one slowly, as it is a tricky pattern. Once mastered, though, it smokes! Try it with all dead notes, also. (Make the first and last notes of each group of sixteenths dead notes instead of Es.)

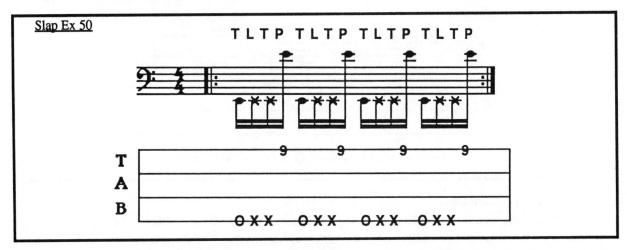

Here's yet another example of how you might use left-hand dead notes in a pattern:

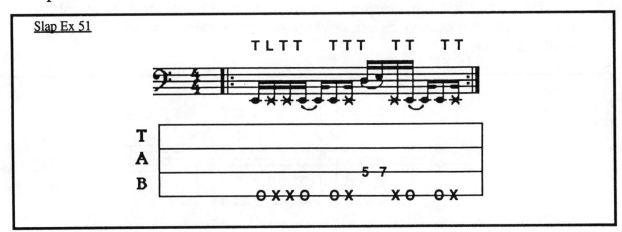

Let's analyze something about that last pattern. Look at the Es that are tied together. One modification you could make to this pattern that is actually pretty natural is to play left-hand dead notes in place of the tied (second) E. It would look like this musically:

The next thing we could do is to make the eighth-note Es in the middle of the second and fourth beats into sixteenth-note Es followed by left-hand dead notes (sixteenths also). It would look like this:

By making these modifications, we have created a pattern that does a lot of alternating between the left and right hands playing dead notes. Doing this will help you develop more coordination and rhythmic capabilities with the right and left hands.

Here are a few more examples using left-hand dead notes. Some of the patterns will be modified as above. You should experiment with your own variations, as well.

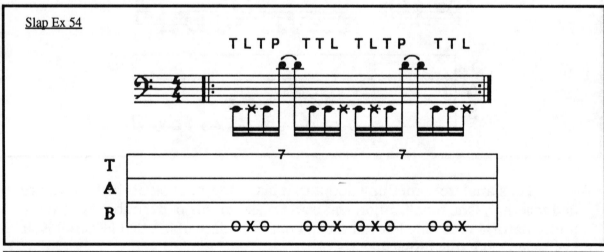

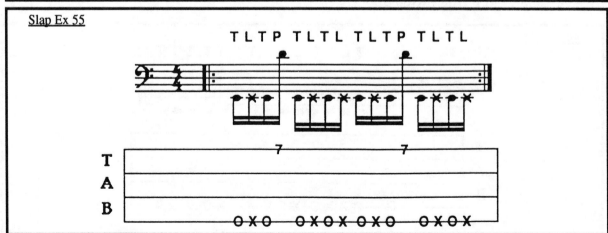

Slap Ex 56

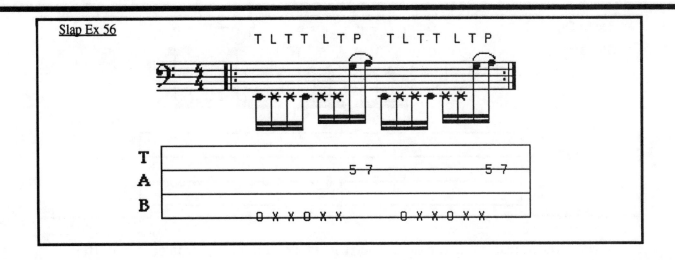

Slap Ex 57

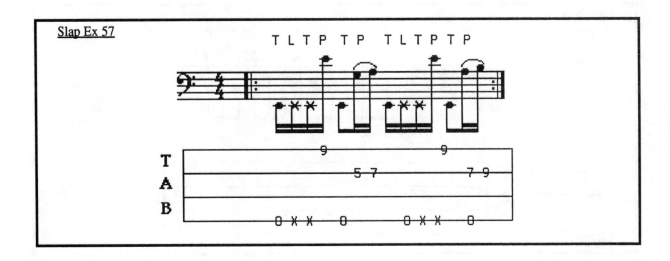

Slap Ex 58

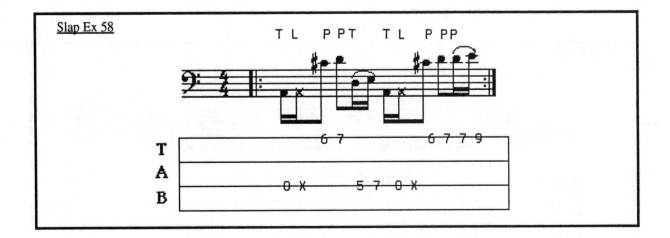

Now that we know all this stuff, let's check out a few *trick* techniques to help "spice things up." Try doing a half-step slide into an octave pattern like this:

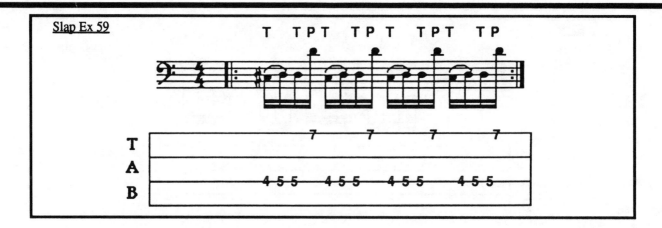

How about using the open A-string as a pedal tone to this octave pattern:

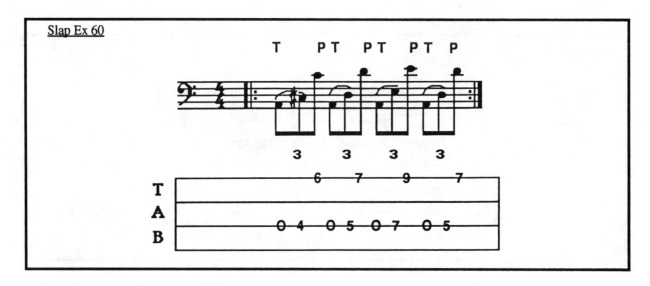

What about going up to the third (F♯) in the bass instead of always going down to the D in this pattern:

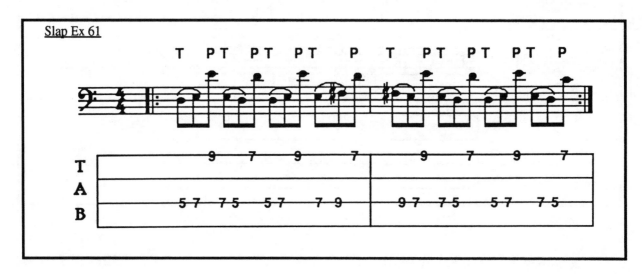

We've talked about a number of different techniques in this chapter. It's up to you to use all of them to your best advantage. Following are a few pages of slap-and-pop lines I have written that use most of the techniques we have discussed. I have included fingering recommendations that are comfortable for me. You should try these as well as others that may work better for you.

It's time for you to use what you have learned. If you just skipped through all of the examples to get to all of these lines, GOOD LUCK! If, however, you have worked your way up to this point, use these lines to help you learn *even more* about the slap playing techniques. Find the best ways for you to play them.

Also, make variations on what I have written. It's not written in stone, you know!! The key thing to remember is......get nuts!! The slap style is a very aggressive and percussive playing style. It just screams for you to play the hell out of it!! Listen to players like Mark King of Level 42, Jonas Hellborg, Marcus Miller, and of course Stanley Clarke for examples of guys who burn at slap playing. Listen and learn. That's the best way to improve your own playing and to begin developing your own style.

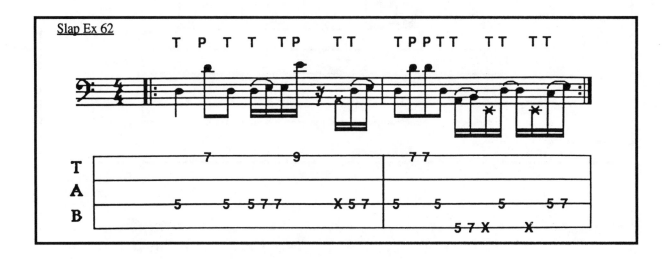

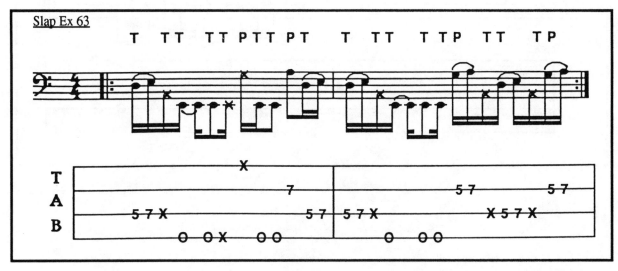

Slap Ex 64

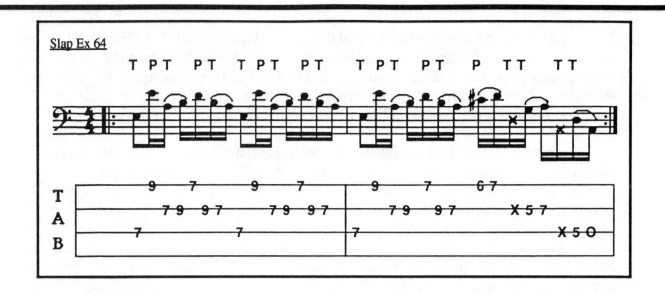

Slap Ex 65

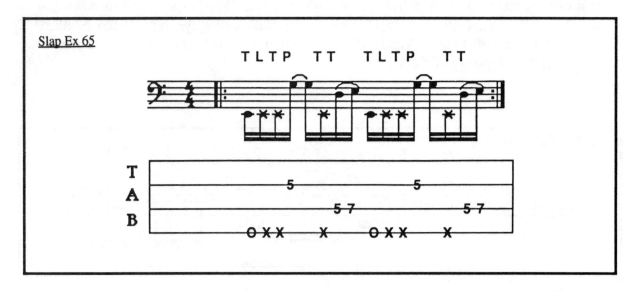

Slap Ex 66

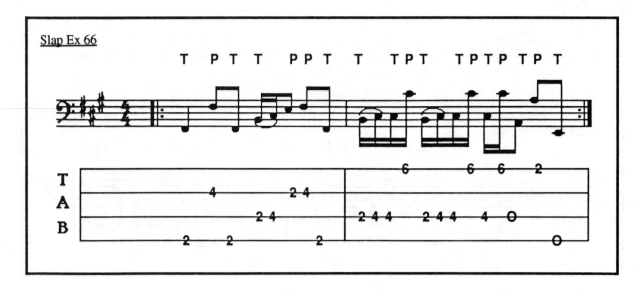

Slap Ex 67

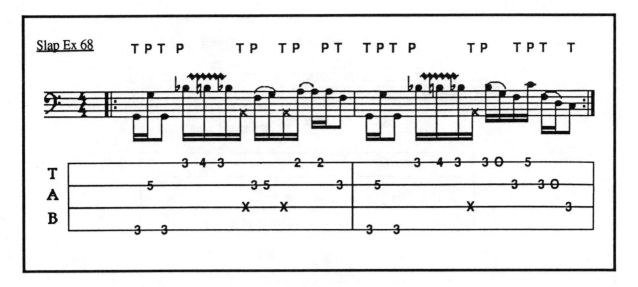

Slap Ex 68

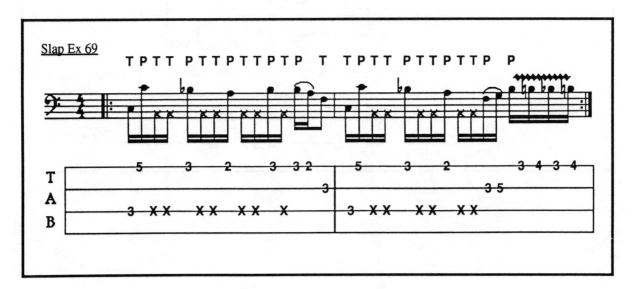

Slap Ex 69

87

Slap Ex 70

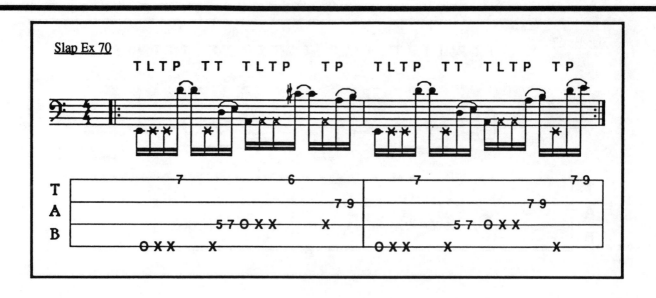

Slap Ex 71

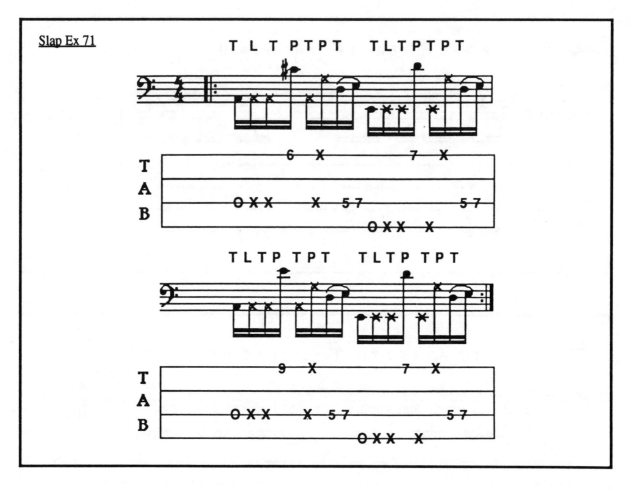

Slap Ex 72

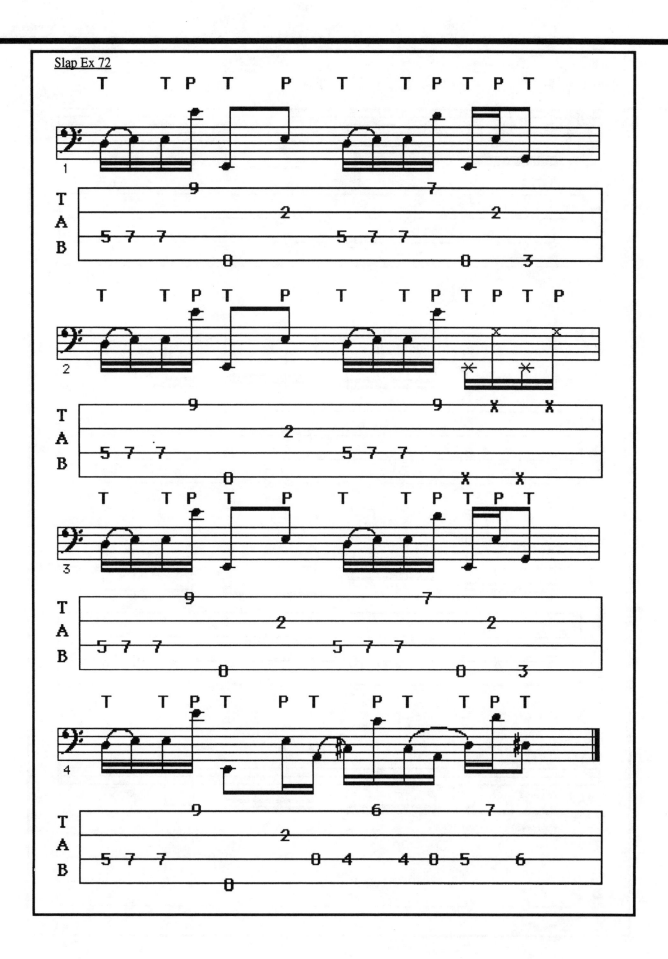

Slap Ex 73

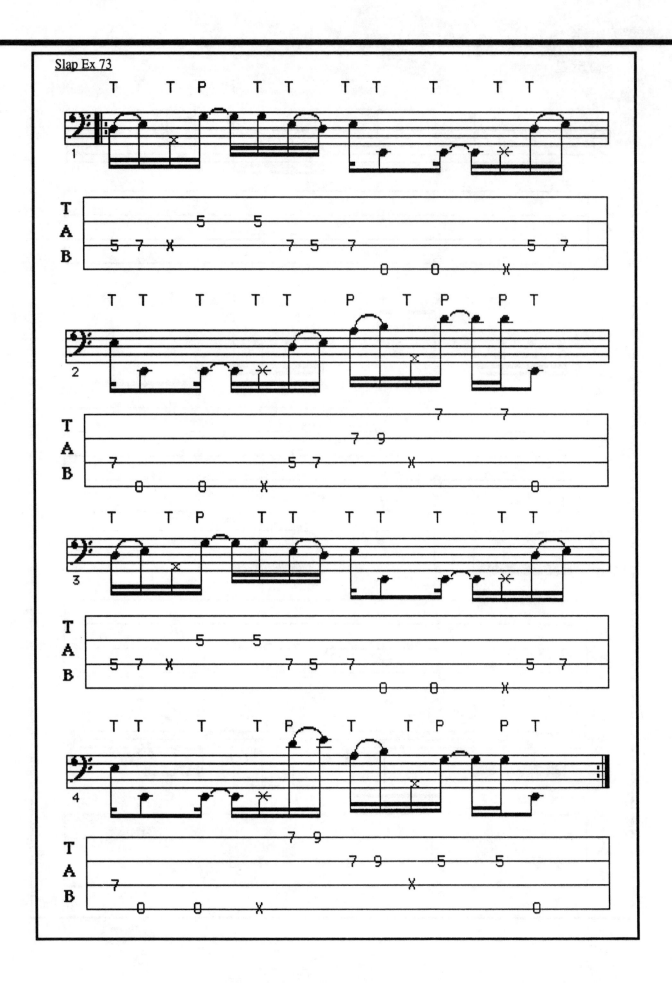

Right-Hand Hammering

Thanks, Eddie. That's the first thing that anyone must say when first learning the right-hand hammering technique, whether it be for guitar or bass. Thanks to Eddie Van Halen for making this playing technique so popular. Since he first popularized this playing technique in the late '70s, it has become a very important part of rock guitar playing. It has since become a very important part of contemporary rock bass playing.

While the technique is usually viewed as a "flashy" or "showy" technique that would be used merely as a show-stopper or attention grabber, it can also be used as a serious part of any bass player's repertoire of techniques. Listen to how players like Stuart Hamm and Billy Sheehan have used this technique in a very musical sense, without abandoning the context of the songs they are playing. It is a very useful technique to have available, should you need it.

First, we will learn the basic technique and concept for playing right-hand hammer-ons using four fingers of the right hand. Of course, there will be plenty of exercises to drill the technique into your head. (With all of these exercises, you must think I'm a health and exercise fanatic! Sure I am....... Aren't all musicians?) Then, I'll write out a number of lines and ideas for you to go off on your merry way into the land of improvisation with your new-found knowledge to rise to superstardom, or at least have a good time! Let's do it.....

RIGHT-HAND TECHNIQUE ....

The right hand is used to do hammer-ons and pull-offs of notes on the fretboard either above or below the left hand. By doing this in conjunction with hammer-ons and pull-offs by the left hand, you will be able to play sweeping lines covering large intervals, as well as play those very quick lines.

To hammer on and pull off notes with the right hand, slide the right hand up the neck to the area where it is to play. When you do this, the right thumb should slide right up the top edge of the neck and act as a counter-balancing force against the hammering and pulling off by the right-hand fingers.

A note is *hammered* with the right hand by bringing your right-hand finger over a fret and firmly pressing down the string to sound out a note. It may take some practice to get a feel for the right amount of pressure. You will learn how to hammer notes with fingers one through four (the thumb is generally not used, except in special cases) on the right hand.

A note is *pulled off* with the right hand by fretting a note with the left hand, then hammering a note above it with the right hand, then performing a pull-off similar to the way you would normally do it with a left-hand finger. You can either pull the right-hand finger up towards your body, or push it down towards the ground to do the pull-off. I prefer to pull up towards the body. You should experiment with both to determine which way feels best and allows you the most control over your right hand.

A note can also be pulled off from one right-hand finger to another right-hand finger. This takes a great deal of control and strength in each of the right-hand fingers. We will have some exercises to help develop the necessary strengths.

LEFT-HAND TECHNIQUE ....

One might think that in a chapter called "Right-Hand Hammering" that the left hand has little to do. Oh, how wrong one would be!! The fact is, the right hand is simply imitating a technique that we have been doing with the left hand for quite some time: hammer-ons and pull-offs. We do it in straight bass playing techniques, and we do it in slap techniques. Now we're just going to expand it to include the right hand.

The basic job of the left hand is simply to hammer on and pull off notes in conjunction with the right hand. So, be sure that your hammer-on and pull-off skills are pretty good. They will only get better when you incorporate the right-hand hammering technique into your "tool box." You should be prepared to hammer on and pull off notes on the same string, as well as those that lie on different strings (i.e., octaves, thirds, typical double-stops...).

It is very important to develop the technique so that there is no volume or tone difference between notes played with the right hand or the left hand. They should all sound the same. With practice, you will find this to be fairly simple. Don't be afraid to get into this and just "man-handle" these bass lines. This can be a pretty aggressive technique, so don't hesitate to reach down and grab these notes! Make 'em count!! Let's play somethin'.......

RIGHT-HAND HAMMERING ....

The first thing we'll do is learn how to play a series of hammer-ons and pull-offs using both the right and left hands. Use this opportunity to develop some coordination between the two hands.

In the following exercise, the B note is played on the D-string with the first finger of the right hand. The A note is played on the D-string with the fourth finger of the left hand. To begin, play the A as you would a normal note by picking it with your right hand. Then, reach up with the right hand and hammer on the B using the first finger of the right hand. Be sure it is a good, solid-sounding note, similar in tone to the A that was played before it. That is how you hammer on a note with the right hand.

The left hand should still be holding down the A with the fourth finger. Next, while still holding down the B (it should still be ringing), pull off the B with the first finger of the right hand to the A (fourth finger of the left hand). Be sure that the pull-off is clean and smooth sounding. For reference, try hammering on the A and B using only the left hand. The right-hand hammering method should sound the same. Here's what it looks like:

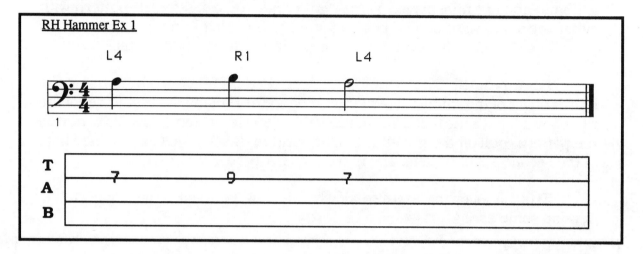

NOTE: The "L4" stands for left hand, fourth finger; and the "R1" stands for the right hand, first finger. (L3 is L.H., third finger, etc.....)

Now, try repeating that type of pattern over and over. You should only "pick" one note, and that is the first one (A). The rest of the notes are to be played by hammering on and pulling off with the right hand (first finger). Again, make sure that both your rhythm and tone are consistent from note to note.

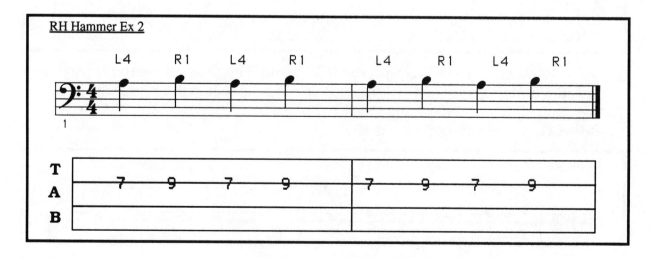

Before we start talking about using all four fingers of the right hand to hammer on and pull off, let's concentrate on the first finger of the right hand and getting used to this whole method of playing.

Probably the most common use of the right-hand hammering technique is to play a repeating pattern of either three eighth-note triplets or four sixteenth notes. Let's take a look at these two ideas for a little while.

The three eighth-note triplet idea involves two notes that are played by the left hand and one note played by the right hand. You can start the pattern with either the left or right hand. Let's first start with the left hand. The three notes we will use are G, A, and B on the D-string (5th, 7th, and 9th frets).

First, pick the G with the right hand, then hammer on the A using the fourth finger of the left hand. Next, hammer on the B using the first finger of the right hand. That's the first three notes of the exercise written below. To continue the pattern, pull off the B with the right hand to the G. The G is the first note of the second set of triplets. The notes are G-A-B-G-A-B-G-A-B-G......

Try the following exercise slowly; and, as you feel more comfortable, develop some speed.

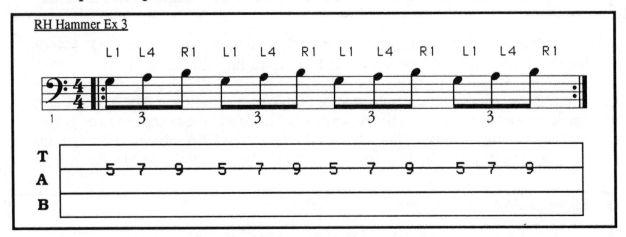

Now, let's try starting with the right hand. The first note is the B played with the first finger of the right hand. Pull off to the A (fourth finger, left hand), then pull off to the G (first finger, left hand). Repeat the pattern as B-A-G-B-A-G-B-A-G..... Here's what it looks like:

There is another way to play the pattern starting with the right hand. That is to play the B with the right hand, pull off to the G (first finger, left hand), and then hammer on to the A with the fourth finger of the left hand. Repeat the pattern as B-G-A-B-G-A-B-G..... Here's what it looks like:

Practice each of these eighth-note triplet patterns until you have them down. Be sure you have them down well, because here comes an exercise that uses all three of those combinations, plus a couple of minor variations on them. This should be a fun exercise, but go slowly at first and be sure you are playing the right notes in the right order, as this exercise tends to go back and forth between notes. Play the D and E notes on the A-string. And notice that some of the G notes are also played on the A-string as well as the D-string.

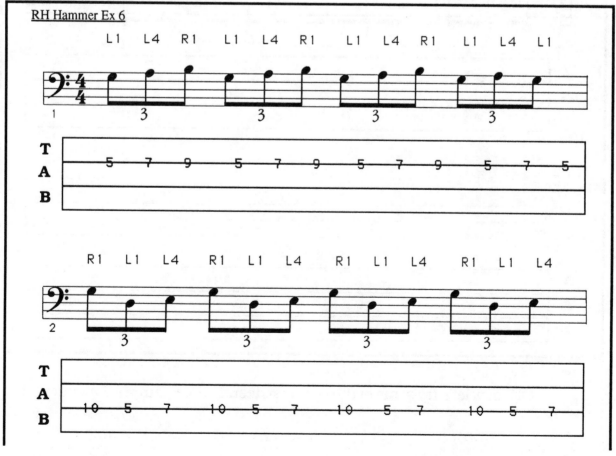

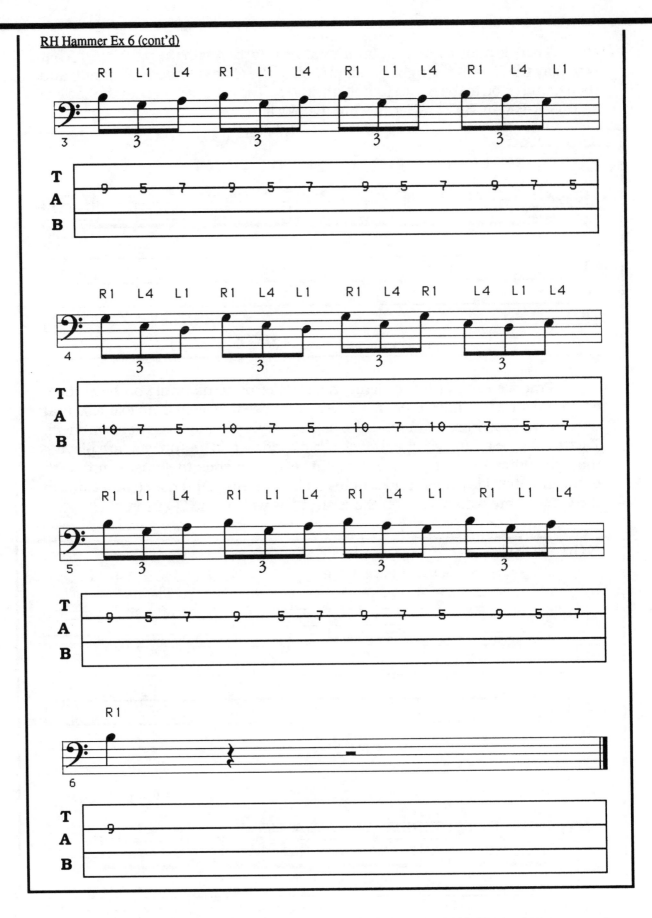

OK, now let's try some of those four sixteenth-note patterns I mentioned before....

As with the eighth-note triplet patterns, the sixteenth-note patterns can be started with either the left hand or the right hand. Let's do some that start with the left hand first.

Play the first note (G) by picking it with the right hand. Hammer on the A with the fourth finger of the left hand, then hammer on the B with the right hand (first finger). Pull off the B back to the A. That's all four notes of the pattern. Here's how it looks in print:

The other way to start the pattern with the left hand is to play the A first, pull off to the G (all left hand), then hammer on the B with the right hand, and pull off to the G. The G and A are all left hand, and the B is the right hand. Here's how it looks:

To start with the right hand, hammer on the B with the right hand, pull off to the A (left hand), pull off to the G, then hammer on the A again with the left hand. That's B-A-G-A-B-A-G-A..... Here's what it looks like:

Another way to start with the right hand is to hammer on the B, pull off to the G, hammer on the A, then pull off to the G again. It looks like this:

Man, I hope you did your homework on those sixteenth-note patterns because here comes an exercise that will make you work if you didn't! It uses only patterns that start with the right hand. Have fun....

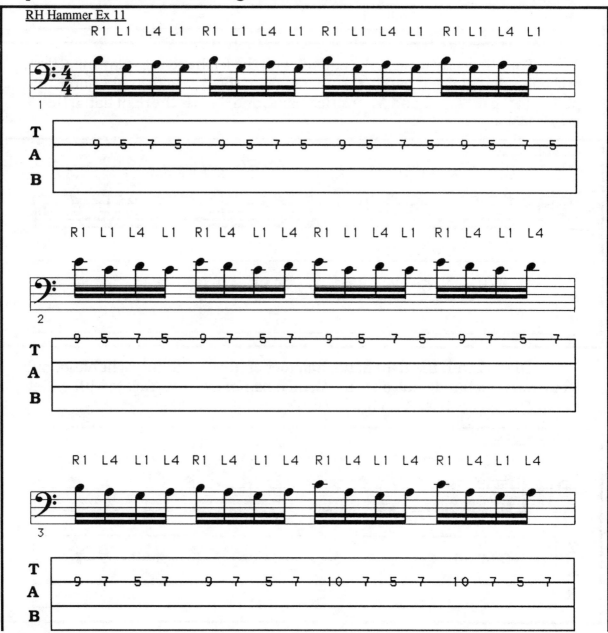

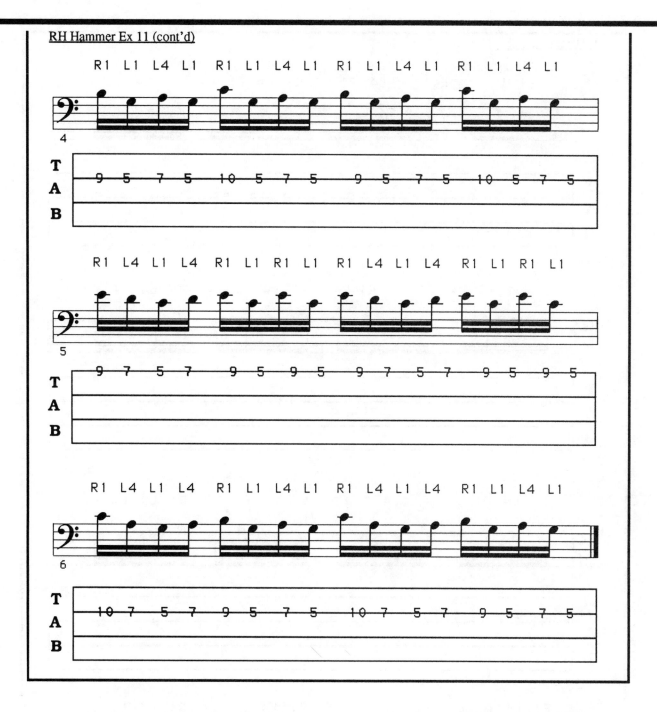

OK, now here's a little finger twister that covers all of the sixteenth-note patterns we've been talking about. The purpose of this exercise, as well as the previous exercise, is to get you used to the idea of changing between patterns without "stumbling." That way, down the road, you can create some really challenging lines and not be limited by what you cannot physically play. Try this on for size....

RH Hammer Ex 12

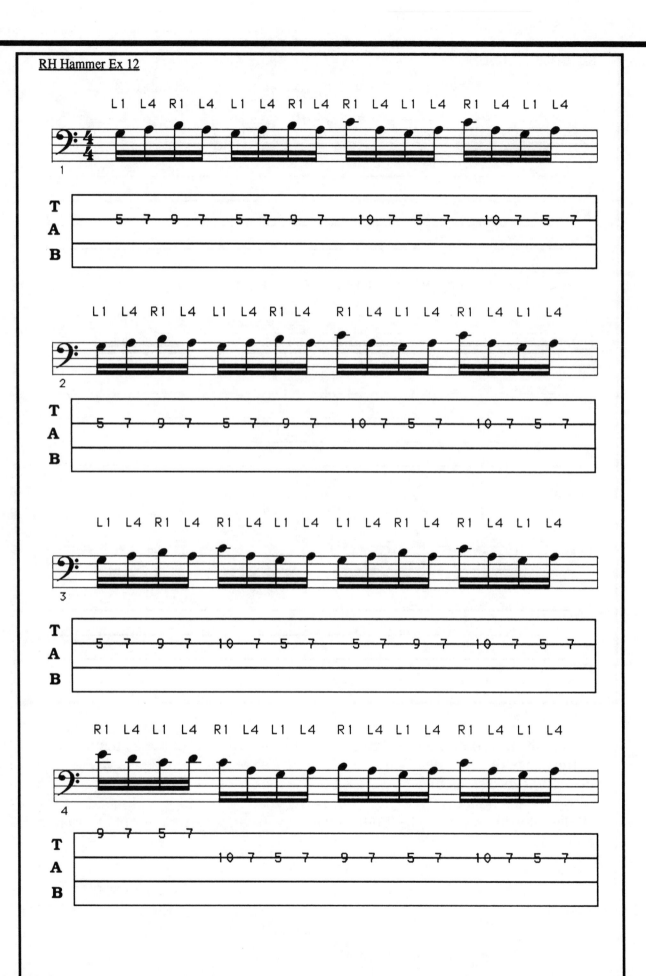

100

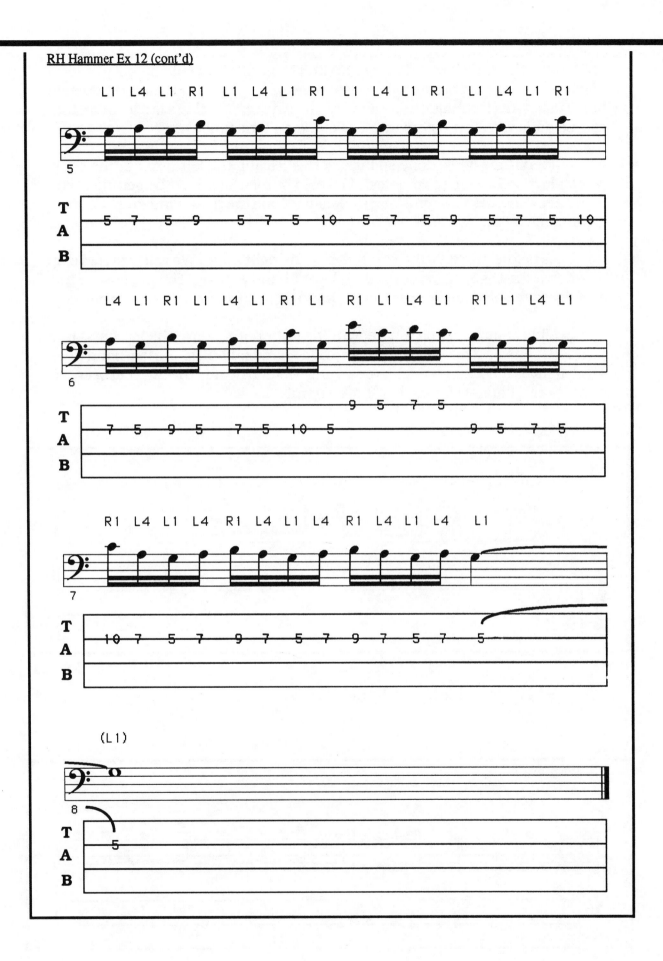

Don't be afraid to *noodle around* with a bunch of different notes of your own to make up some of your own patterns. What you've learned so far is enough to begin using this technique in your everyday playing. But, there is a lot more that can be done with this technique! So, let's get a little fancy.....

Everything we've done so far involves leaving the left hand in the same place playing the same two notes. If I were your left hand, I'd be getting pretty bored about now!! Let's try moving the left hand and the right hand to create some moving melodies.

As before, use only the first finger of the right hand. We will first move up and down the D-string to get used to the left hand moving. The purpose of this exercise is to gain control over the left hand as it walks up and down the neck.

After hammering on a note with the right hand, move the left hand into position for its next note(s). Then do the right-hand pull-off to the left-hand note. The left hand must move quickly, changing position during the time between the right hand's hammer-on and pull-off. Try this.....

Let's have a little fun with this idea......

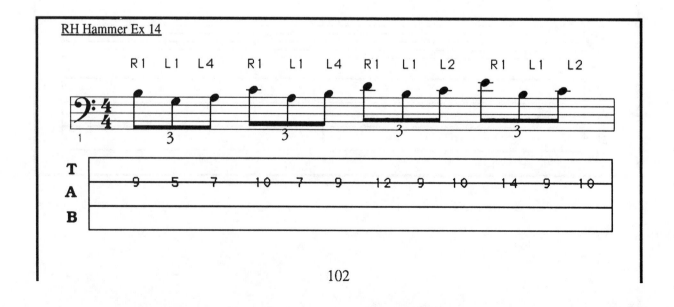

RH Hammer Ex 14 (cont'd)

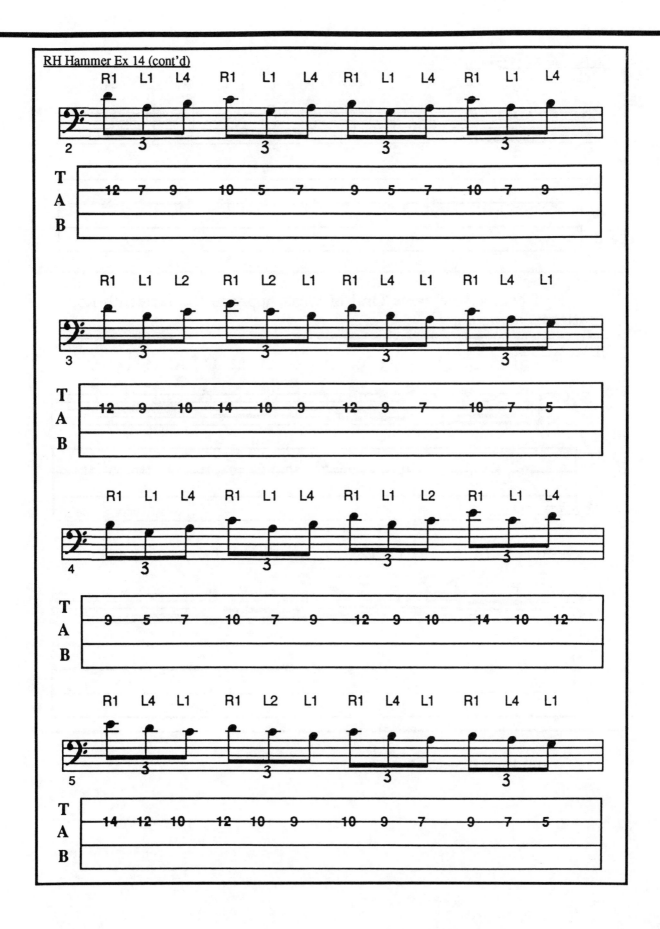

Of course, the same kind of ideas apply to the sixteenth-note patterns, as well....

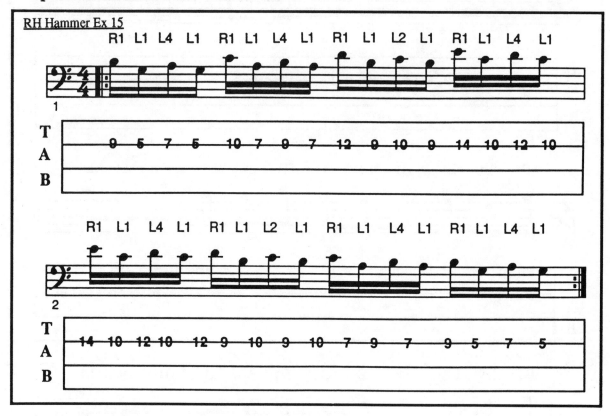

And then there's always......

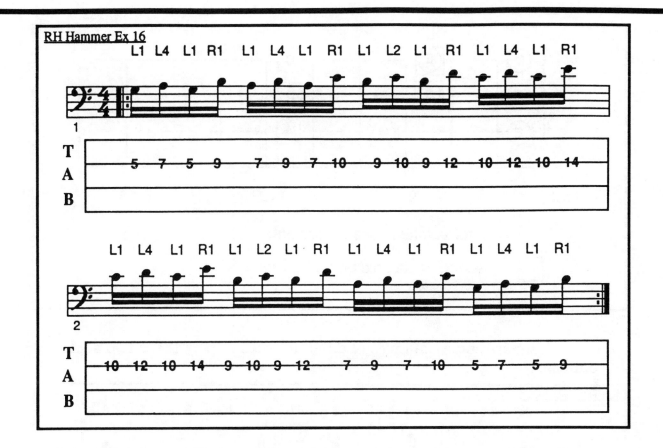

RH Hammer Ex 16

SCALES AND SCALE PATTERNS ....

Some of the most creative right-hand hammering lines come from the use of scales in combination with the right-hand hammering technique. The right-hand hammering technique can be used to run through scales at a very quick pace and also cover larger intervals. Let's take a look at some of the possibilities. (Be sure to check out the section on scales in this book for more scale patterns and ideas!)

Perhaps one of the most-used scales in popular music, the **pentatonic scale** is a derivative of the minor scale. It consists of five notes of the minor scale—the first, minor third, fourth, fifth, and seventh notes. When using the right-hand hammering technique to play scales, you are really playing two of the scale positions in one line. Here's a diagram of the E pentatonic scale. The circles represent one scale position, while the squares represent the next higher position. Notice that they overlap. We can use that to our advantage here.

105

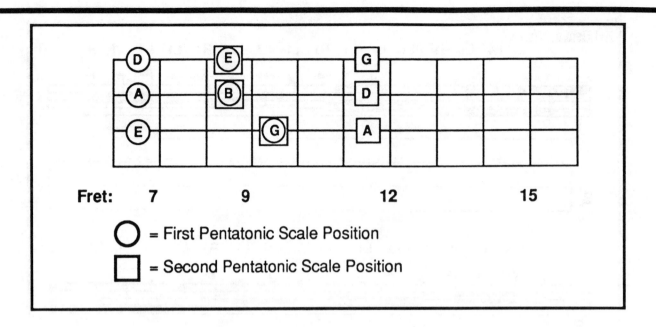

Fret: 7   9   12   15

○ = First Pentatonic Scale Position

□ = Second Pentatonic Scale Position

Here are some examples of different ways to play these two scale patterns.

RH Hammer Ex 19

R1 L1 L4 L1 R1 L1 L3 L1 R1 L1 L3 L1 R1 L1 L3 L1

Now, let's add the next higher pattern into the picture. Here's a diagram to show you where the scale positions fall:

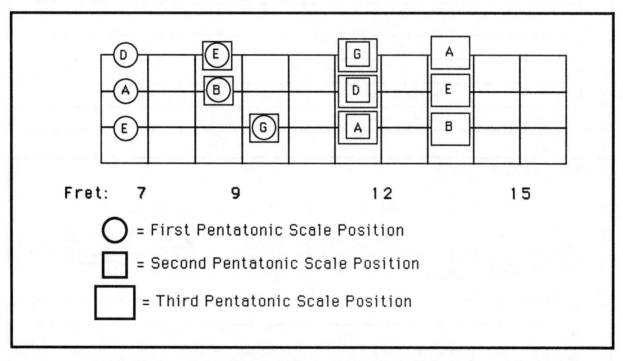

Fret: 7   9   1 2   1 5

○ = First Pentatonic Scale Position

□ = Second Pentatonic Scale Position

□ = Third Pentatonic Scale Position

Now we'll play all three patterns together. First, we'll combine all three into one melody line that climbs up through all three. Here are a few examples:

RH Hammer Ex 20

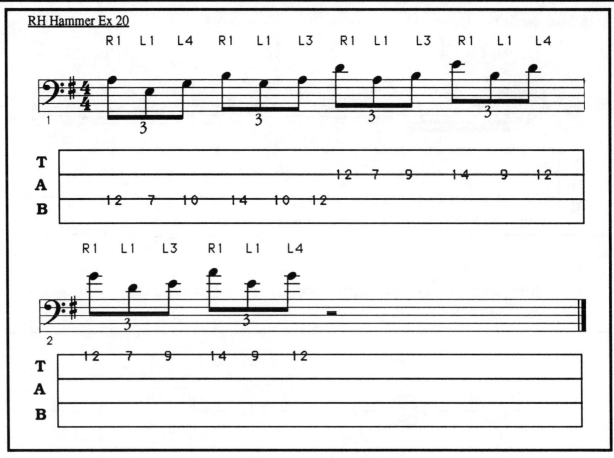

RH Hammer Ex 21

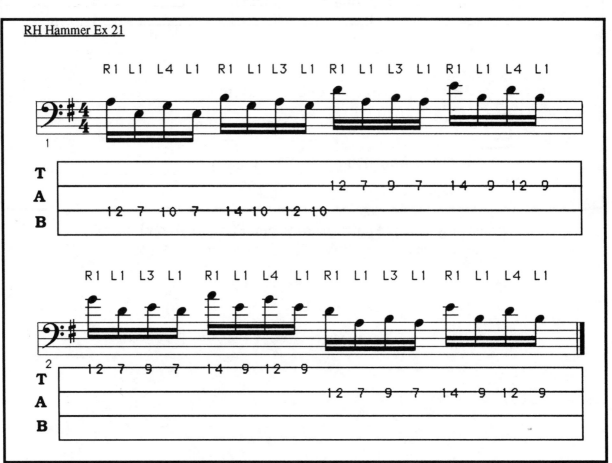

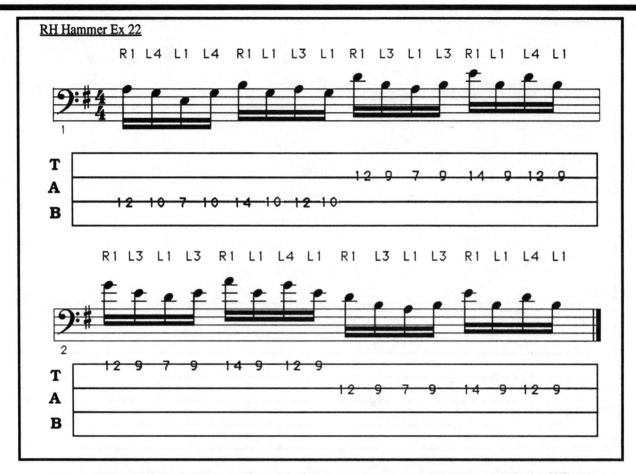

RH Hammer Ex 22

Getting the idea? You should also experiment with your own melody lines, as there are many, many more than just the few that I'm showing you.

Now, here's another approach to the scale-pattern idea. Play up the first and second positions, then come down the second and third positions. Like this.....

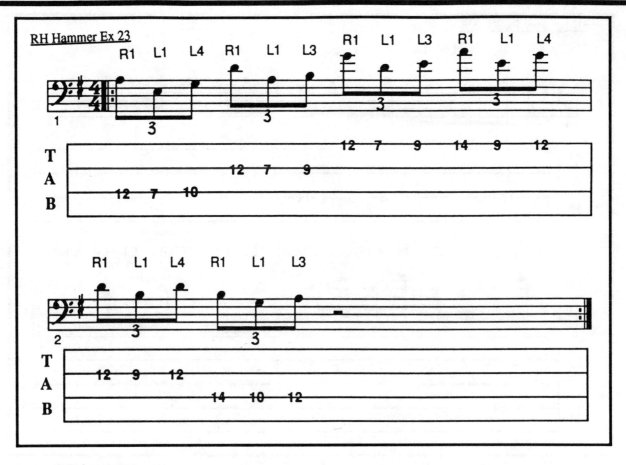

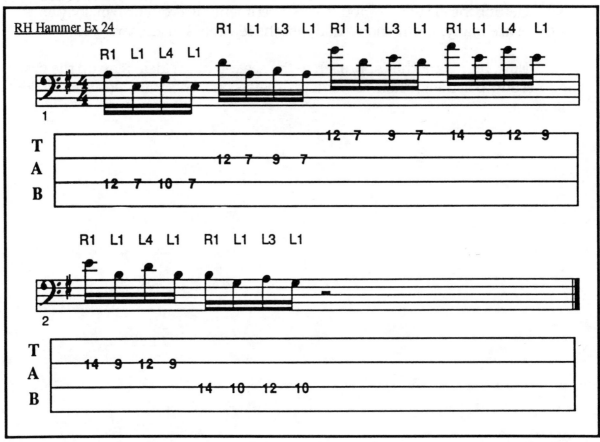

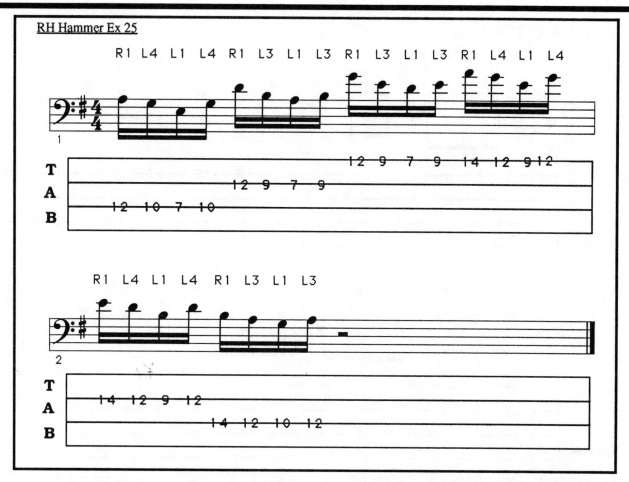

RH Hammer Ex 25

This idea can be expanded to cover all positions of the scale from one end of the neck to the other. Here's an example of the pentatonic scale expanded to cover one full octave of the fretboard. This is an eighth-note triplet pattern. Try it on your own with some other eighth-note triplet patterns, as well as some sixteenth-note patterns.

RH Hammer Ex 26

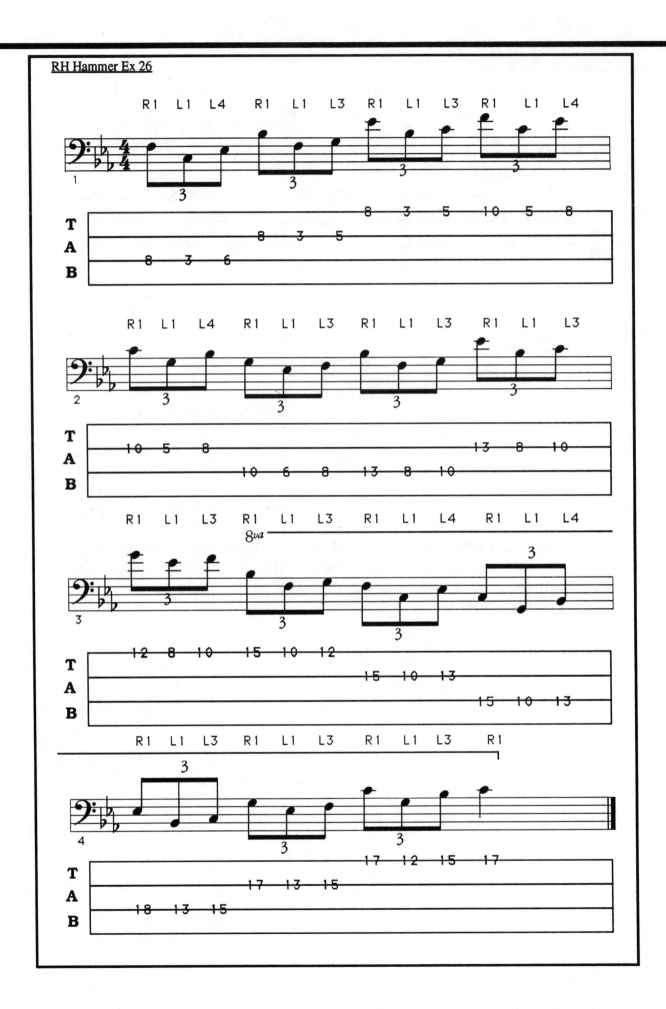

112

The same type of patterns can be used for major scales, minor scales, harmonic minor, etc..... Here's an example of the C major scale expanded to cover the entire fretboard (or at least one full octave's worth).

Experiment with some other scale patterns, as well as musical patterns. There are many variations on every pattern you can think of, so play around with some different ideas and you'll find that, by doing so, you are able to create a large number of useful patterns!

USING MORE THAN ONE RIGHT-HAND FINGER ....

Now this whole time, while we have been playing these different ideas, you've had three other fingers on your right hand that could have been used to help create wider intervals between notes, help play more notes in a pattern, and even play the patterns more comfortably.

There are actually a couple of ways to play with more than one right-hand finger. One way is to use any one of the four right-hand fingers to play a particular note (i.e., don't always use the first finger of the right hand, but use others as well). The other way is to play more than one note at a time, using two or more right-hand fingers at once. Let's talk about the first way—using all four fingers to play notes as you please.....

As far as the technique goes, each finger of the right hand is used in the same manner. So, in the following exercises, you should use the same technique for all four fingers as you have been using for the first finger.

First we'll look at the technique of using four fingers on the right hand, then we'll get into some examples of melodies and lines that may be played.

The first exercise will help get you used to the idea of using four fingers on the right hand. You will use your left hand to play the notes G, G♯, A, A♯ on the D-string. The right hand will play the notes B, C, C♯, and D on the D-string, pulling off to the left-hand notes. Use the first finger of the right hand to play the B; the second finger to play the C; the third to play the C♯; and the fourth to play the D. The exercise is to be played up (B-G-C-G♯-C♯-A-D-A♯) and then back down, without repeating notes. The idea is to get the right-hand fingers to go 1-2-3-4-3-2-1-2-3-4-3-2-1, etc....

Practice this exercise over and over by repeating the phrase until you feel comfortable with it. Here's what it looks like in music and tablature:

114

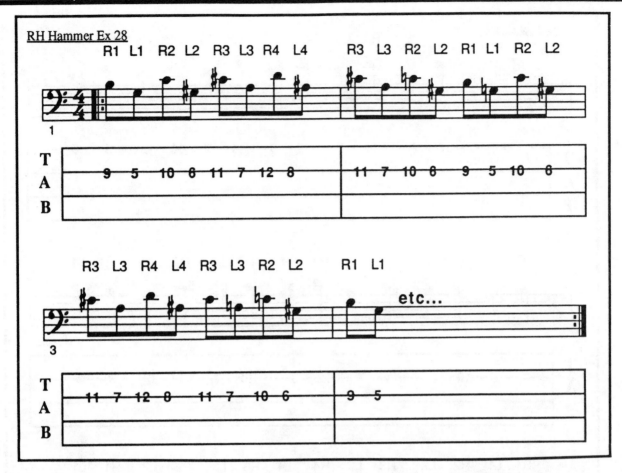

RH Hammer Ex 28

How's that right hand feel? If you're like me, it hurts! The first and second fingers are usually used to picking the strings, so they're pretty strong. But those third and fourth fingers..... Oh, boy!! They are out of shape. Exercises like this are like sending your fingers to an aerobics class! So, you should approach these exercises carefully. You want to do them as if you were working out at a gym. Don't try to do too much at first. A little muscle-burn is OK; but, when it gets painful, stop and rest a little. Straining your muscles and tendons will only slow down your progress. Remember, slow down and you'll go faster.

The above exercise should also be played on all four strings. Here's an example of how to do that. You can make up your own variations.

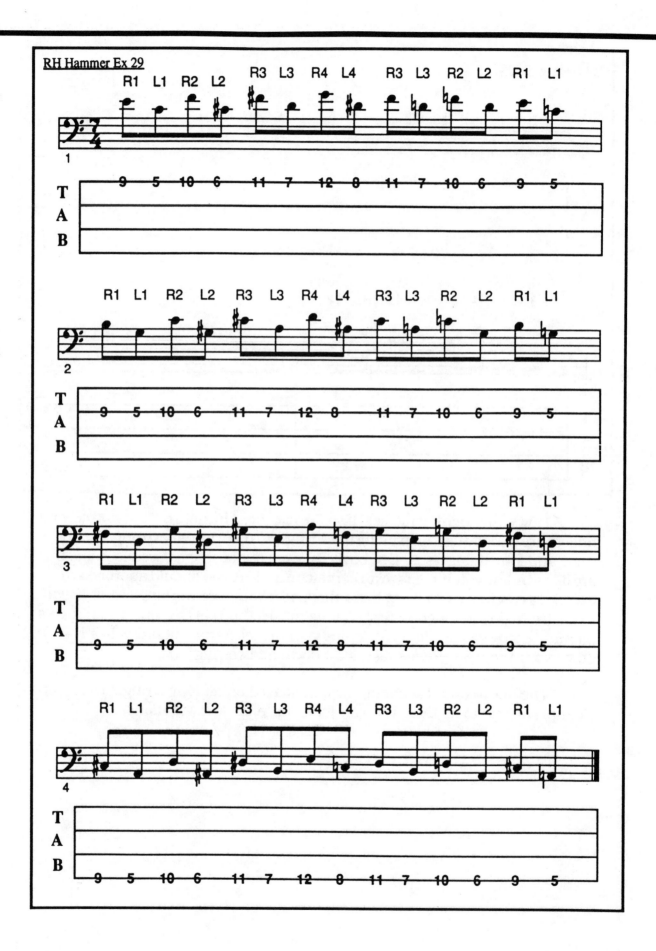

Here's one that's a little trickier because it requires some serious strength in the right-hand fingers. This is a chromatic exercise that is started with the left hand using fingers 1-2-3-4. Then continue the chromatic climb using the right-hand fingers 1-2-3-4. Now, reverse the notes by pulling off with the right-hand fingers 4-3-2-1 into the left-hand fingers 4-3-2-1. Confused? Try it.....

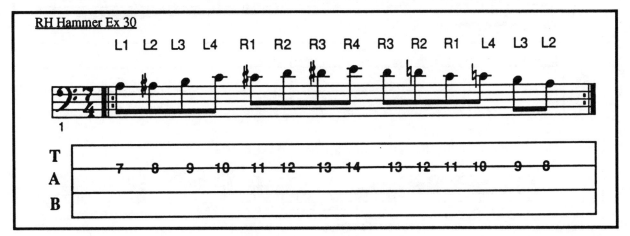

Move that exercise around to some other strings.

Now, we're going to learn some right-hand hammering exercises that, if done regularly, will increase the dexterity and strength in your right hand to allow you to play anything that you can reach. So, I'm going to diagram the patterns and I'll leave it to you to learn how to do them the full length of the neck. Move these patterns around the neck to other positions.

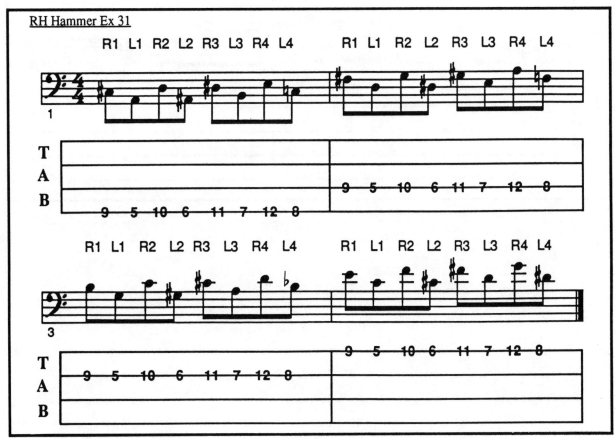

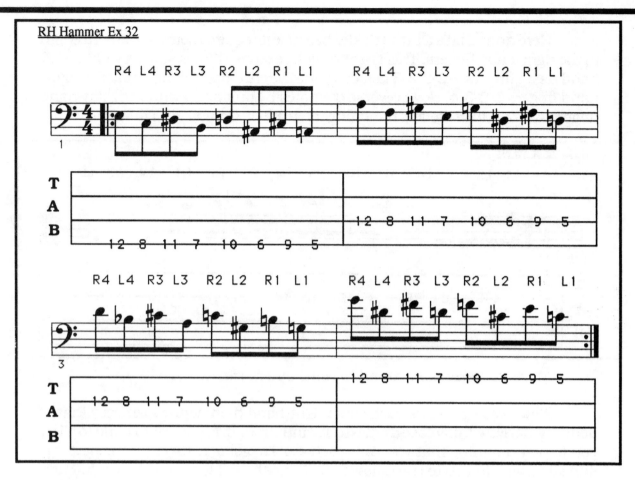

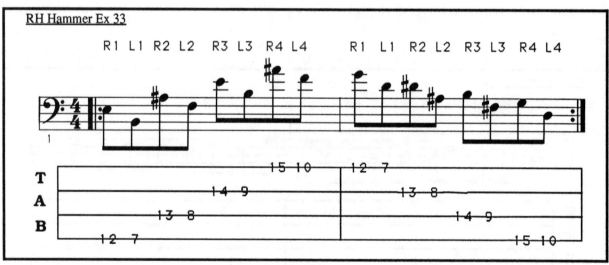

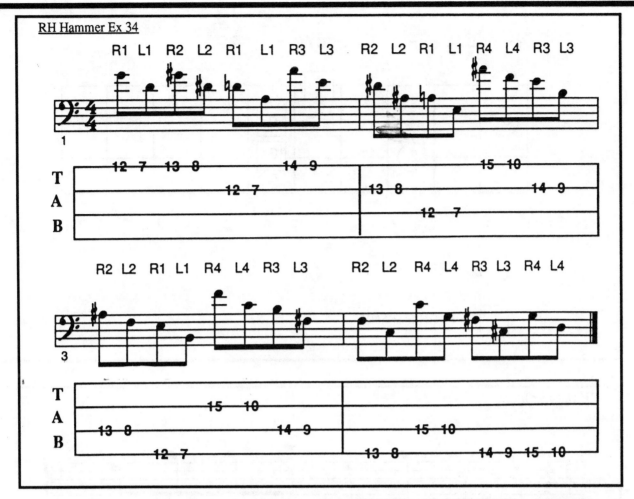

RH Hammer Ex 34

Now that you know how to use all four fingers of the right hand (that is, if they haven't fallen off yet), let's look at some applications of the technique. The first and possibly the most interesting method is to arpeggiate chords in two different inversions with both the right and left hands. (Also, be sure to read the section on chord-tone studies in this book for more ideas!)

Let's start simple. Use the left hand to make a C/E chord (see the diagram below). Now, we are going to arpeggiate by pulling off the notes in a C/G chord with the right hand into the C/E chord of the left hand. Watch this......

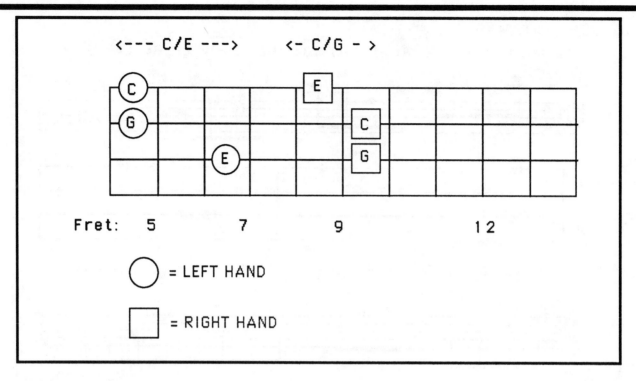

<--- C/E --->   <- C/G - >

Fret: 5   7   9   1 2

◯ = LEFT HAND

▢ = RIGHT HAND

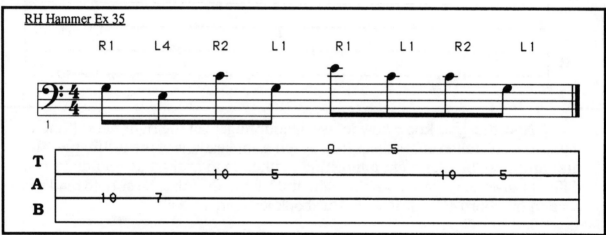

RH Hammer Ex 35

R1   L4   R2   L1   R1   L1   R2   L1

Try it again, this time letting the notes played by the left hand ring throughout the measure. You can create some really interesting chordal effects this way.

Here's an example of a chord progression played with the right and left hands.

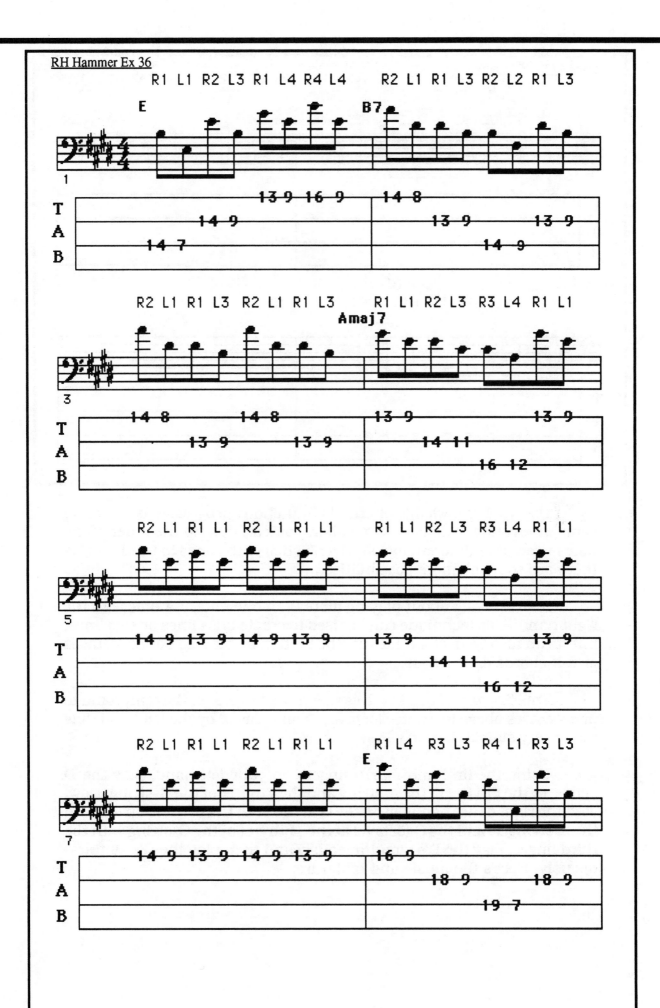

121

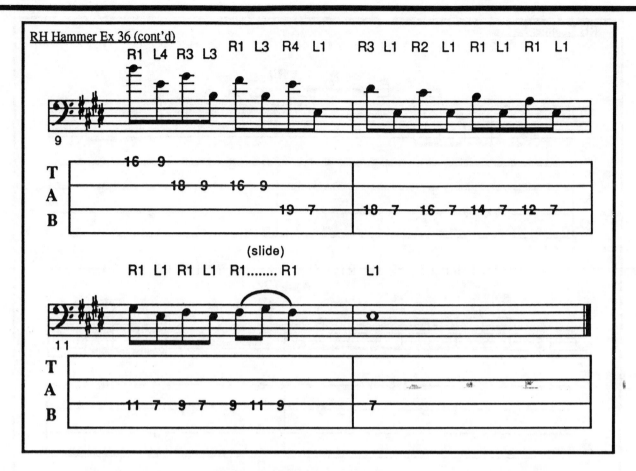

Use your knowledge of chords and chord progressions to create some interesting melodies. Remember, you can mix up the order of the notes to create a different melody. Don't stick to the ones in this book, as there are so many more possibilities....

Now let's talk about playing more than one note at a time with the right hand. This technique can be used to create bass lines or solo lines, but it can also be used to "fill out" the bottom by playing double octaves or full chords on the bass.

This first technique involves using two fingers on the right hand to play octaves above two notes (octaves) being played by the left hand. It is really very simple. Let's try it....

Using the first and fourth fingers on your left hand, play the D octave at the 5th fret of the A-string and the 7th fret of the G-string. Now, with the right hand, hammer-on the G at the 10th fret of the A-string with the first finger, and the G (octave) at the 12th fret of the G-string with the third finger. Play the D's simultaneously and then play the G's simultaneously. Here's the music and tablature:

122

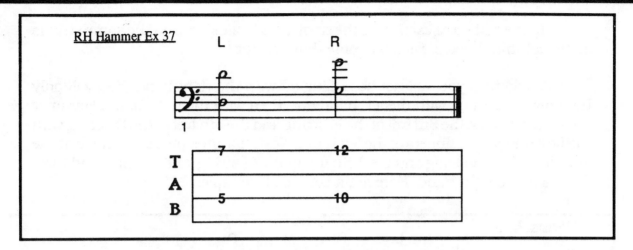

Now try the same thing; but, after hammering-on the G octave, pull-off back to the D octave. Like this....

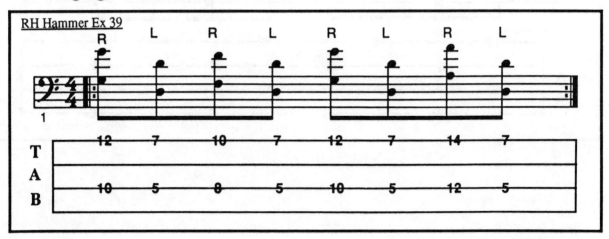

Let's not stop there! Here's an example of a line that could be played using right- and left-hand octaves:

Experiment with different intervals between the right and left hands. That is, in the above exercise, the G octave is a 4th above the D octave; the F is the minor 3rd; the A is the 5th. Try some other intervals to create some different effects.

In the last three examples, the right-hand notes were on the same strings as the left-hand notes. Let's try some that are not.

To do this, you will not be pulling off with the right hand. You will only hammer on octaves with the left hand and then with the right hand. Hammer on the G octave at the 3rd fret of the E-string and the 5th fret of the D-string with the first and fourth fingers of the left hand. Next, hammer on the G octave at the 10th fret of the A-string and the 12th fret of the G-string with the first and third fingers of the right hand. Here are a couple of examples:

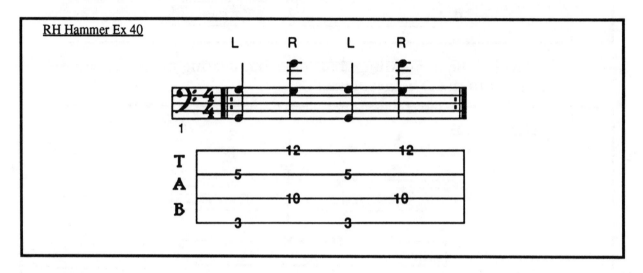

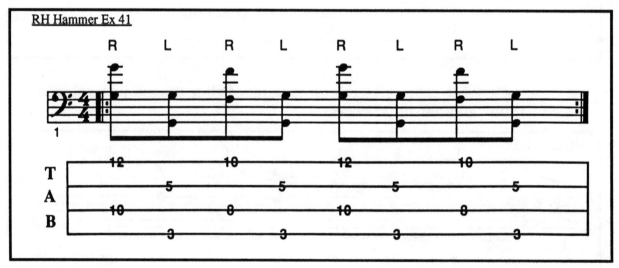

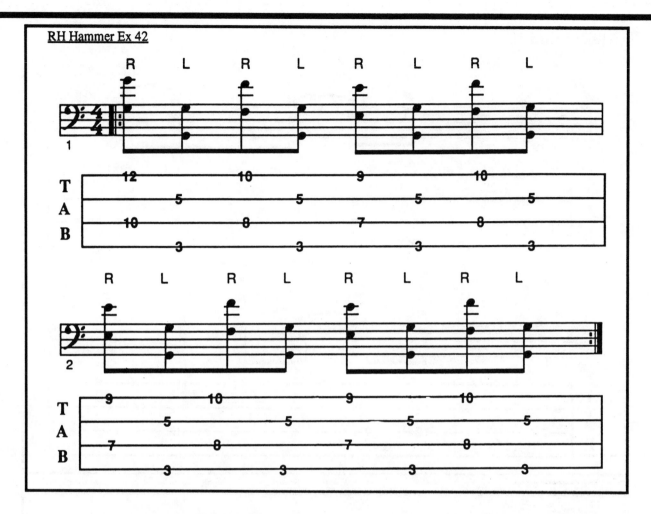

RH Hammer Ex 42

You can also use this technique to play intervals other than octaves. You can play thirds, fifths, fourths, etc....whatever your little heart desires! Use the same technique as above with the right and left hands. However, always use the fingerings that are the most comfortable and easiest for you to use. If you use these ideas in the middle of a song or a bass line, keep in mind which fingers are needed for the notes that are played prior to the right-hand hammering phrase as well as those played after the phrase.

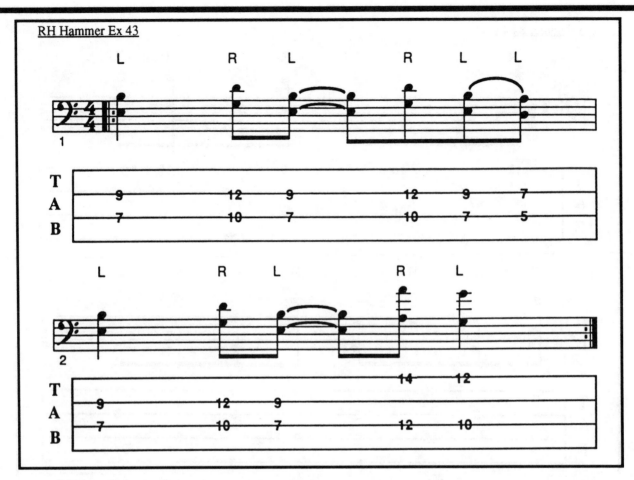

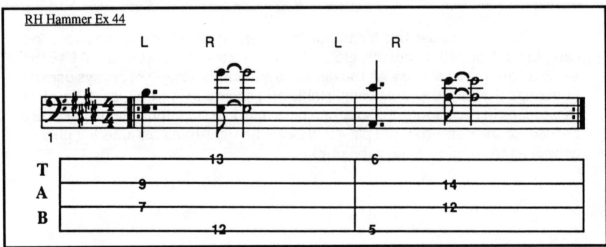

OK, there's just one more thing we need to talk about. All this time, maybe you noticed that the right hand was always playing notes that were located higher up the fretboard than the left hand. Is this the only way to use the right hand to play notes? No way!! The only things I know to be "forever" are death, taxes, and the pain in my back from moving bass amps!!

You may be asking, "How do you play notes with the right hand lower on the fretboard than the left hand?" You just do it! (Don't you just love a smart aleck?) Try this.....

Using the first and second fingers of the left hand, play the F♯, hammer on the G, hammer on the A with the first finger of the right hand. Pull off the A to the G, pull off the G to the F♯. Now, pull off the F♯ to the E, playing the E with the first finger of the right hand (your right hand should now be lower on the fretboard than your left hand). Pull off the E to the D, playing the D with the first finger of the left hand. Hammer on up to the E, played with the third finger of the left hand. Hammer on up to the F♯, played with the first finger of the right hand. Pull off to the E, pull off to the D. Now, reach down with the right hand and hammer on the lower D at the 5th fret of the A-string with the first finger of the right hand. Here's the music and tablature:

This idea can be used to play long melody lines, as well. Here's a melody that I have used in a bass part I wrote. It uses this same technique. I like it—hope you do, too!

RH Hammer Ex 46

128

OK, class..... time for the final! Actually, this is your chance to test yourself. I have written out some different examples of how you may use the techniques we have been talking about in this section.

The most important thing, though, is this: Use these musical exercises to help develop and solidify your ability to play using the right-hand hammering technique. The real goal, however, is for you to go out and create your own melodies and uses for the technique. Incorporate it into your own style as you see fit.

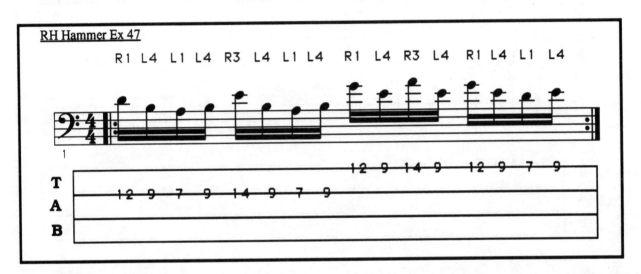

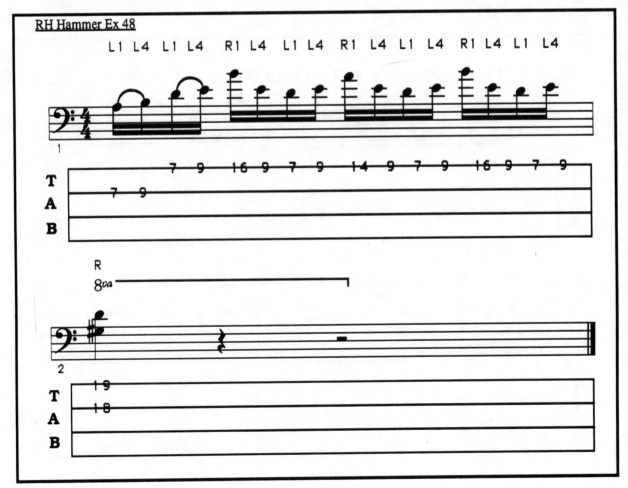

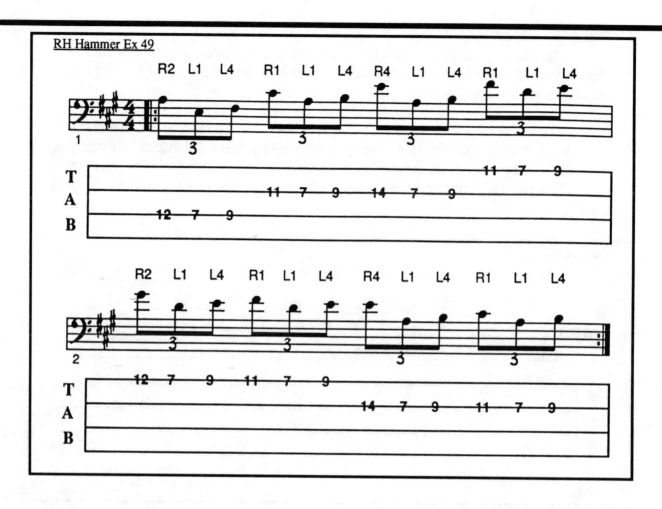

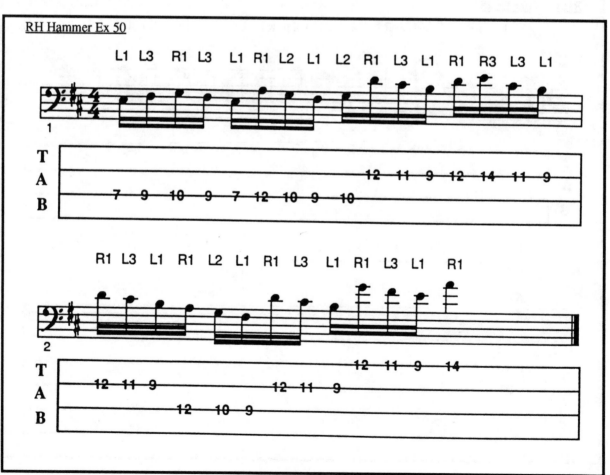

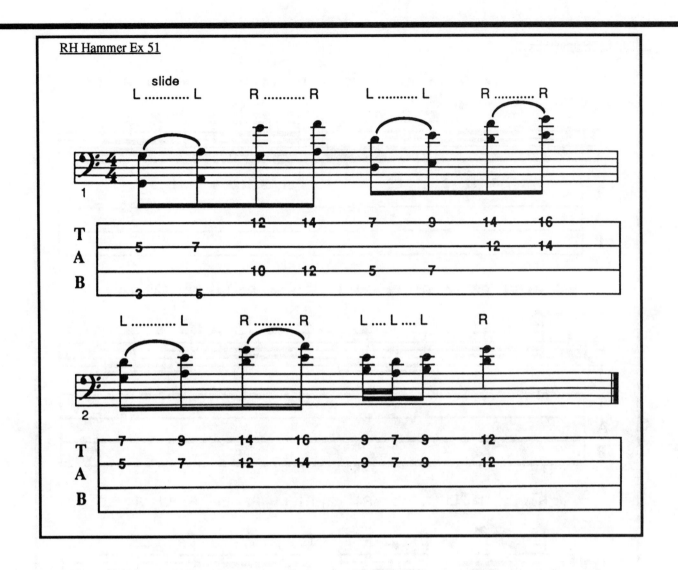

RH Hammer Ex 51

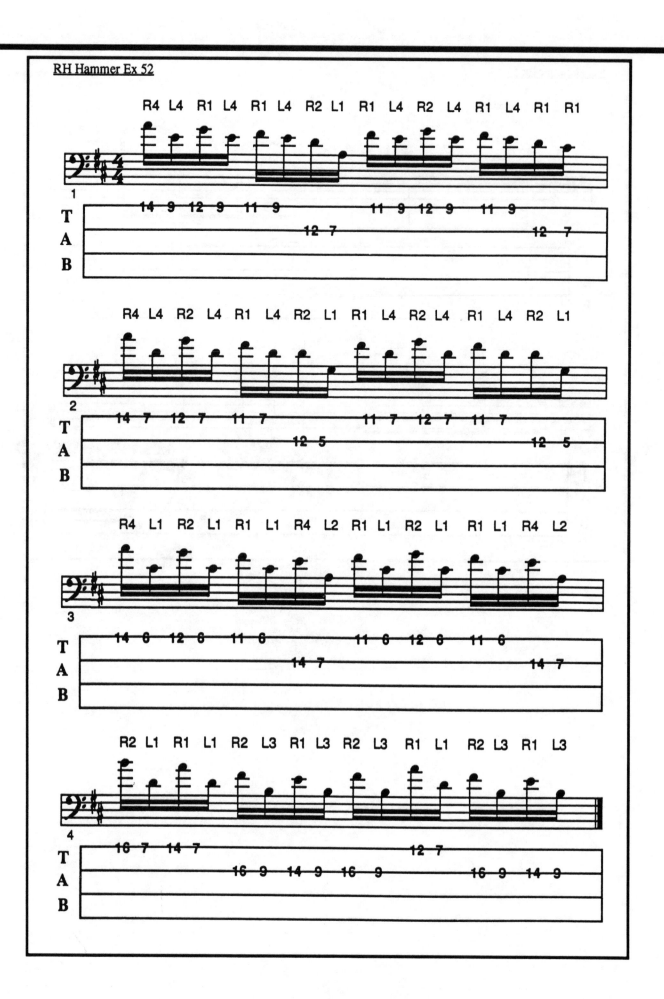

RH Hammer Ex 53

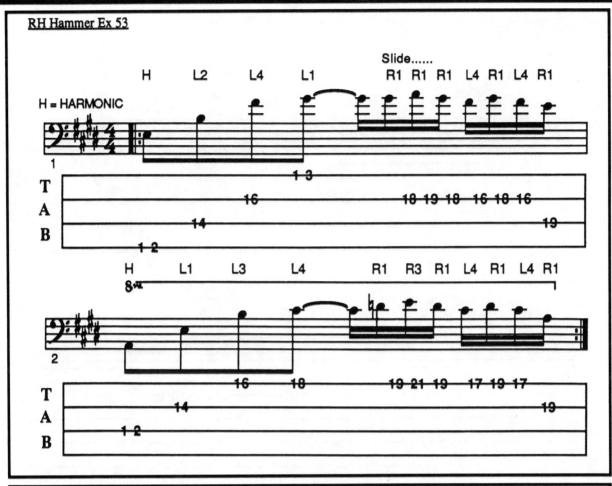

RH Hammer Ex 54

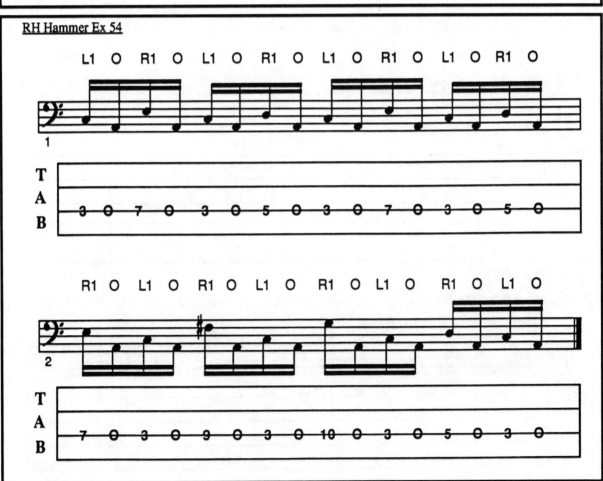

133

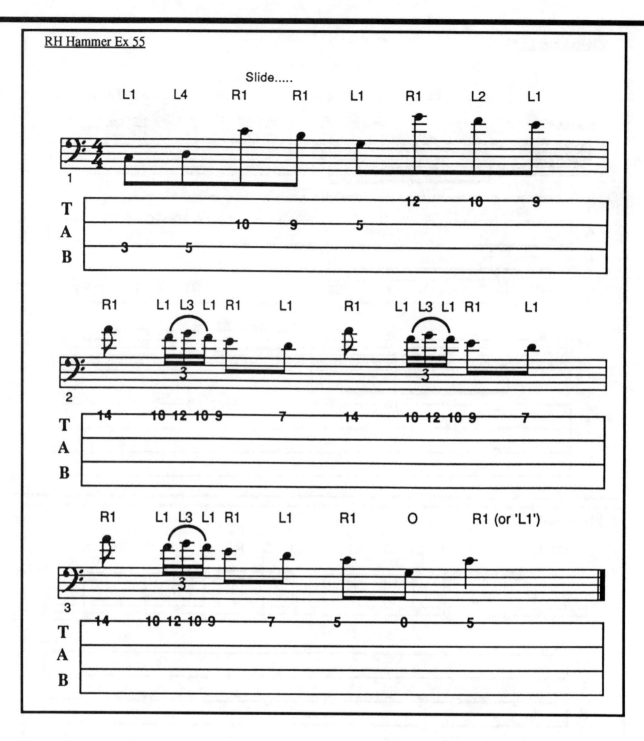

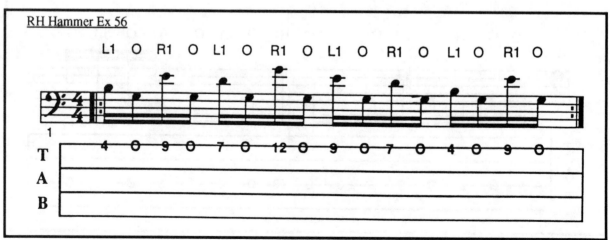

RH Hammer Ex 57

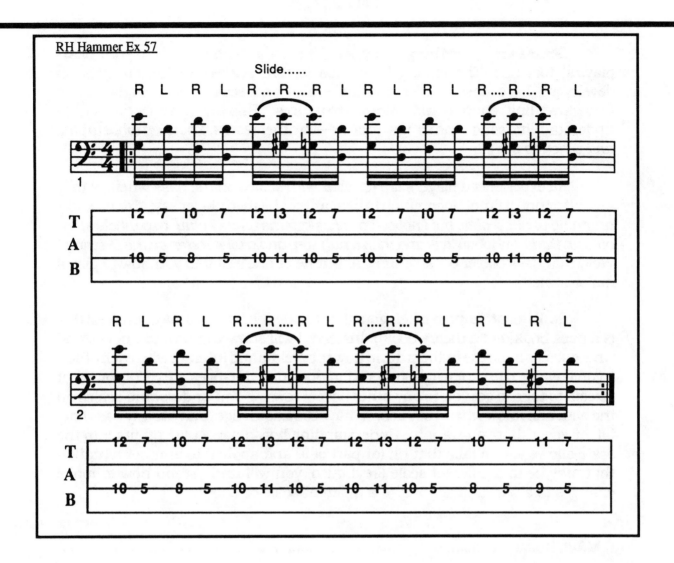

Scales

Scales are everything. They are the most important tools in your bass-playing tool box. The reason I say this is that scales are fundamental in developing bass lines. Understanding scales and scale theory leads you to understanding chords and chord structures. This in turn leads you to understanding songs and song structure—in other words, *knowing what to play and when to play it.*

All experienced players are familiar with scales on the bass whether they know it or not. It is not uncommon to hear an established player say, *"I don't know anything about scales, but I notice specific patterns when I play: two whole steps on both the E- and A-strings and then a half step and a whole step on the D-string."* Well, that bass player doesn't know it, but he or she just told you how to play a major scale!

I will not attempt to teach you about scale theory in this section ('cuz this is a bass book, not a theory book!). Instead, I will show you how to understand where scales lie on the fretboard and how they relate and interact with each other. If you have lived in your neighborhood for a long time, chances are you know what streets to take to get you to any other part of town. If you understand scales on the bass and know where they lie, you have the knowledge to create any bass line, fill, or effect that you want to. Understanding how a particular riff fits into the scale allows you to take that riff (or part of it) and apply it to another situation that may be in a different scale (key). Also, you will understand how to make changes to a part and adapt it to a different scale or chord.

C MAJOR ....

We will start will the C major scale because it has no sharps or flats (i.e., it's simple!). First, let's say a few things about scales in general:

a)   The notes in a major scale are determined by the series of intervals between those notes. A major scale is always W-W-H-W-W-W-H, where W = whole step and H = half step.

b)   A scale does not necessarily start and end at its root. A scale can be played starting and ending at any note in that scale, on any part of the fretboard.

c)   When you are playing in a specific scale, you are playing the notes in that scale, not just a particular finger pattern.

With those things in mind, let's take a look at the way a C major scale lies on the fretboard. We will do this by looking at the scale in each of the different mode positions for C major. For the purposes of this book, a mode position will be defined as the position on the fretboard that contains the current mode. In each case, the scale will be shown in two ways: 1) scale tones only, starting and ending at the tonic, as determined by the mode; and 2) all scale tones in that same position, regardless of starting and ending notes (called "entire position"). This will allow you to see how the scale falls on all strings on all frets. Without further delay, the C major scale.....

C Eleven (C11) Chord Tones 1-(3-5)-b7-9-11
(Due to the nature of the Eleven Chord the 3 and 5
are not played.)

CHORD-STRUCTURE CHART ....

Following is a chord-structure chart for 21 different chord types, not all of which have been covered in this section. Review the chart and use it for reference if ever you're not sure of the chord tones in a particular chord.

Major	1,3,5
Minor	1,♭3,5
Major Sixth	1,3,5,6
Major Seventh	1,3,5,7
Dominant Seventh	1,3,5,♭7
Minor Sixth	1,♭3,5,6
Minor Seventh	1,♭3,5,♭7
Augmented Fifth (+5)	1,3,♯5
Diminished Fifth (-5)	1,3,♭5
Diminished Seventh (dim.)	1,♭3,♭5,♭♭7
Dominant Seventh ♯5 (7+5)	1,3,♯5,♭7
Dominant Seventh ♭5 (7-5)	1,3,♭5,♭7
Minor Seventh ♭5 (m7-5)	1,♭3,♭5,♭7
Add Nine	1,3,5,9
Six Nine 6(9)	1,3,5,6,9
Major Nine	1,3,5,7,9
Dominant Nine	1,3,5,♭7,9
Minor Nine	1,♭3,5,♭7,9
Dominant Seventh ♯9 (7+9)	1,3,5,♭7,♯9
Dominant Seventh ♭9 (7-9)	1,3,5,♭7,♭9
Eleven	1,(3,5),♭7,9,11

Song Structure

This section will not be like a music-theory class. Instead, I want to talk about song structure and theory as it applies to contemporary bass playing, since that's what we all do anyway. I will explain things as they relate to the message I am putting across, as opposed to answering all of the questions about "why" theory is the way it is. I want you to be able to take the information in this book (all of it) and apply it directly to musical pieces, ideas, and challenges right away. So, let's talk song structure.

Where do the notes and chords in a piece come from? Well, music is written in a **key.** A key is the scale from which that particular song's notes are taken. Therefore, the piece is taken from a scale. That's very important to remember—we'll come back to it.

The chords in a song are taken from the scale, as well. Due to the relationships between the notes in a scale, *a specific order of major and minor chords can be related to major and minor keys.*

Here are the chords for both major and minor keys. We will look at C major and its relative minor key, A minor:

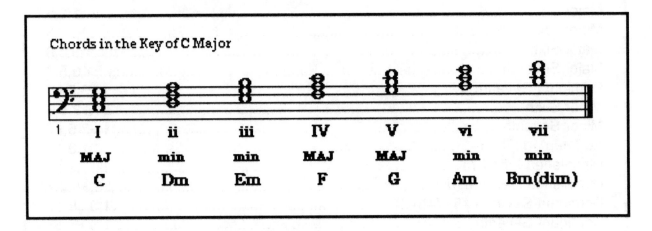

Chords in the Key of C Major

I	ii	iii	IV	V	vi	vii
MAJ	min	min	MAJ	MAJ	min	min
C	Dm	Em	F	G	Am	Bm(dim)

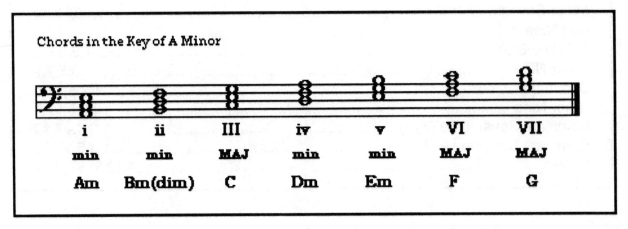

Chords in the Key of A Minor

i	ii	III	iv	v	VI	VII
min	min	MAJ	min	min	MAJ	MAJ
Am	Bm(dim)	C	Dm	Em	F	G

One thing to notice about these two keys is the order of major and minor chords. In a major key, the major chords are the first, fourth, and fifth. The rest of the chords are minor. This order is true for all major and minor keys. You should memorize the order of chords in both major and minor keys.

Also, the chords in a key are often referred to by number, and those numbers are designated using upper- and lower-case Roman numerals. Lower-case numerals indicate minor chords, while upper-case Roman numerals indicate major chords.

Knowing these two orders gives you a tremendous advantage when you approach a piece. Most songs are written **diatonically;** that means that all of the notes (and therefore chords) are taken from the key. This also means that, if you know what key a song is in, and you can play that scale (same as the key)—*ready for this?*—you know all of the notes that can and probably will be played in that song.

Now, before we get too excited, that statement is not always 100% correct; but, if you approach a song with that in mind, you will be way ahead of the game (as opposed to not having any clue as to what is about to happen). Since music is art and is subject to creative license by the composer and those who interpret the music, most rules can and will be broken regularly. But, as I said, knowing which notes should be in a song will make it much easier to learn or to create a part for that song and make the few adjustments necessary to make it comply with the composer's wishes. (It's easier to learn a few exceptions to the rule than to learn everything from scratch.)

In the next section, we will look at developing bass lines using the ideas discussed in this book. It is my belief that strong understanding of scales, chord structure, and song structure, combined with good rhythmic skills and sensitivities, are what good bass players are made of. Learn as much about all of these things as you possibly can and apply them to the best of your ability. It is also very helpful to look at existing pieces and analyze them to understand which notes are played and why.

Developing Bass Lines

A number of things contribute to the creation and development of a bass line. What you feel at the time, what other people are playing, what you know, what you don't know, what you are capable of, what you are not capable of, and sometimes most importantly, what the person who's paying you tells you to play! All of these things contribute. So, with all of that input coming at you, let's get into.....

HOW TO DO IT

Listen. That's not an order, that's the key to developing a bass line. What does the piece need? Listen and it will tell you. Listen to the rhythm. That will tell you what is happening rhythmically. Listen to the chords. They tell you what is happening chordally. And, above all else, listen to the melody. The melody is what everybody is listening to, and you don't want to be stepping all over it!

We spent a whole section talking about different rhythm patterns. It was done with the emphasis on reading, but that doesn't mean that you didn't absorb any of it. Listen to what the other rhythm players are playing and *listen* for the bass rhythm that supports and complements them.

We spent another section learning about and studying chord tones. When you see or hear a specific chord, immediately think of the chord tones that go into that chord. Incorporate those chord tones into your bass line. Now you are supporting the chord changes in a rhythmic fashion. Use other scale tones and passing tones to help "walk" from one chord to another.

At the same time, you are listening to the melody to make sure that you are not stepping all over it, because you are playing 4 billion notes. Pick notes and rhythms that complement the chords and melodies, and everybody will be happy. This doesn't mean you have to play *boring ol' bass parts!* No way! The fun and interesting part is looking and listening for, and ultimately finding, that bass part that stands on its own while complementing and supporting everything else in the song. That's how to do it!

CHORD PROGRESSIONS

We are now going to take a simple look at some fairly common chord progressions and go down a path that explains how to create and develop bass lines for them. First, without even supplying a bass line, here is a basic chord progression called a "1-4-5" chord progression. It is called a "1-4-5" because it uses the #1 chord, the #4 chord, and the #5 chord of the key. In a major key, those chords would all be major chords; therefore, they are all identified using upper-case numerals.

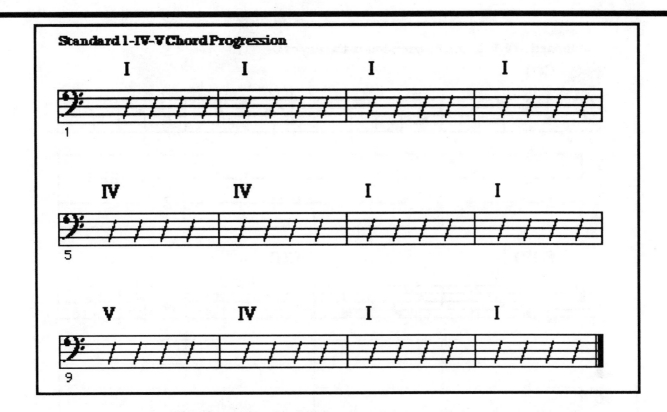

Standard 1-IV-V Chord Progression

Now, let's put a key to this chord progression. For simplicity, we'll use the key of C major. I have also added the chord tones for each chord. Play through them as written. We'll forget about any complex rhythms for a while, and suddenly we have the makings of a song:

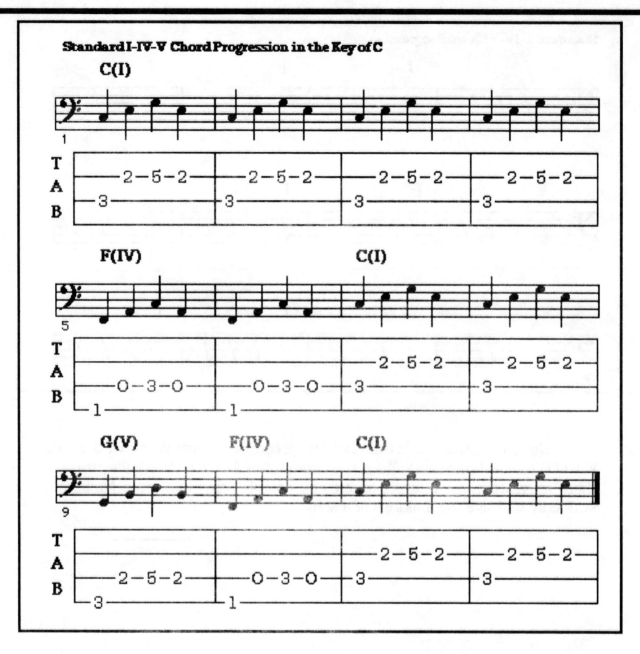

Now, as with everything else in life, there can be variations (exceptions to the rules as previously discussed) to our little chord progression. Play the chord tones for each chord as shown in the following variations:

194

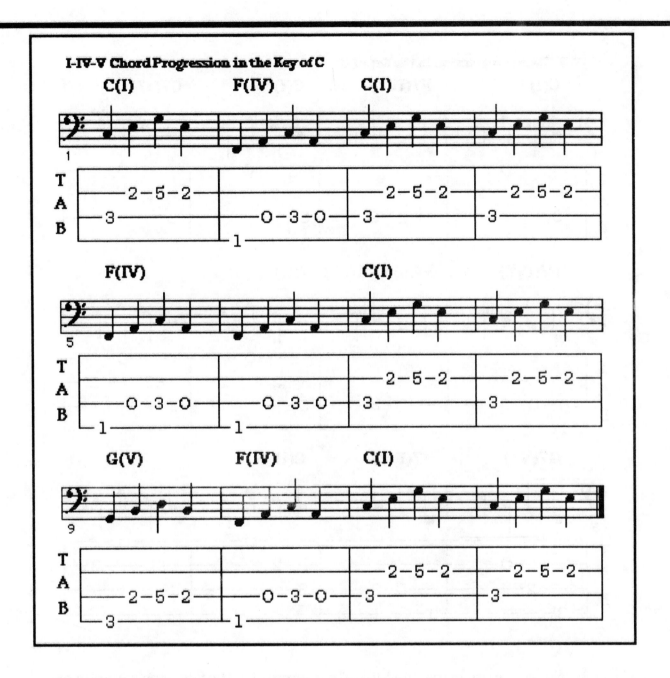

I-IV-V Chord Progression in the Key of C

195

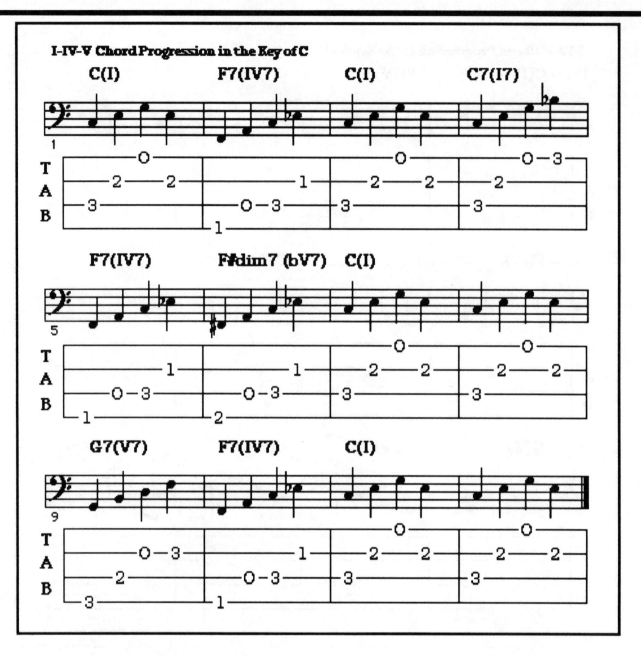

Notice the use of the "iii-vi-ii-V-I" turnaround in the following variation on the I-IV-V progression. It is a very common chord progression on its own!

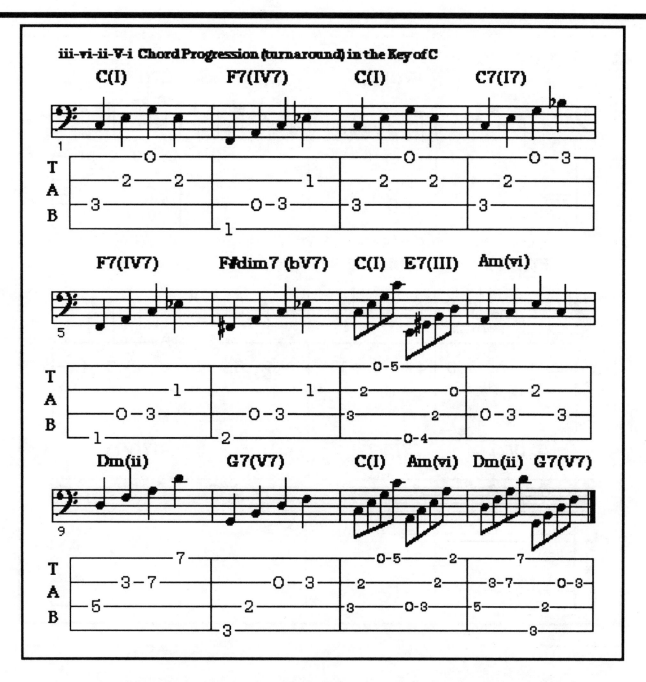

Now it gets a little more interesting as we use the chord tones, scale tones, and a few passing tones to create a bass line that simply "walks" through the chord changes. Thus, we have taken a chord progression (1-4-5), figured out the key (C major), figured out the chord tones for each chord, analyzed some variations, and created a bass line using all of our scale and chord-tone knowledge!

I-IV-V Bass Line in the Key of C

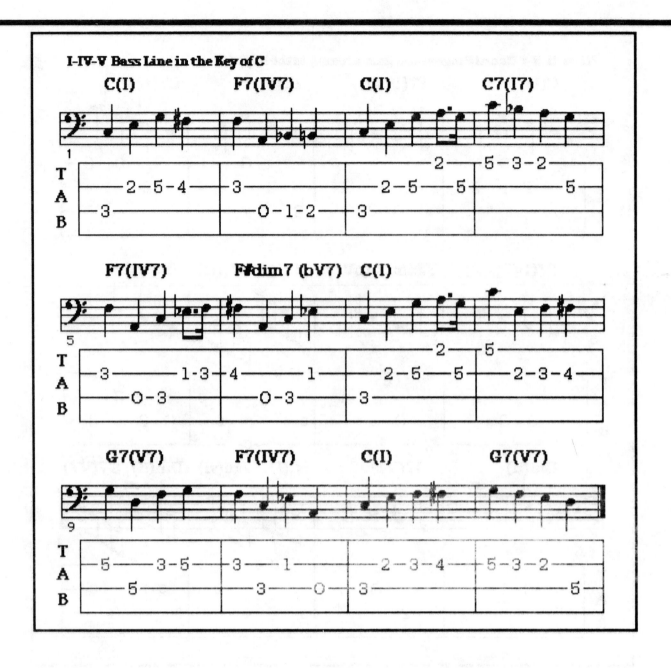

198

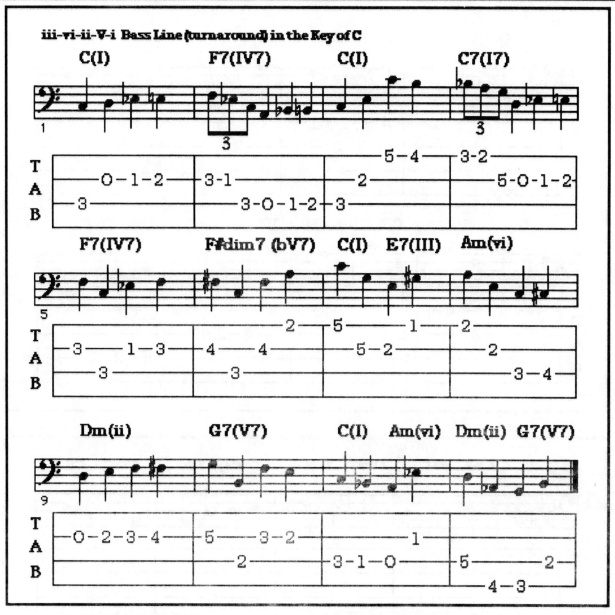

Sometimes, you might really be tested by a chord progression that seems to go in and out of the specified key. It's legal—we're talking "art is music and music is art" here. No problem, though, because we studied our chord tones really hard and are not fooled by anything! Here are a couple of examples along those lines.

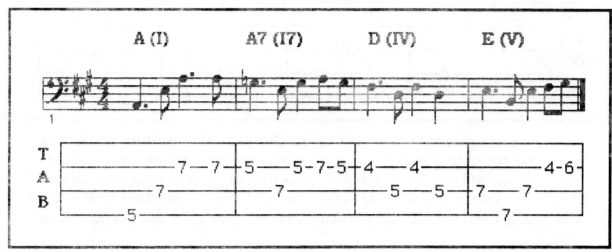

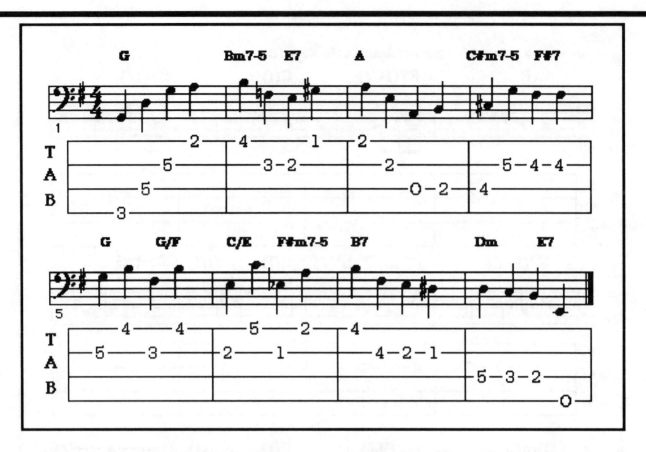

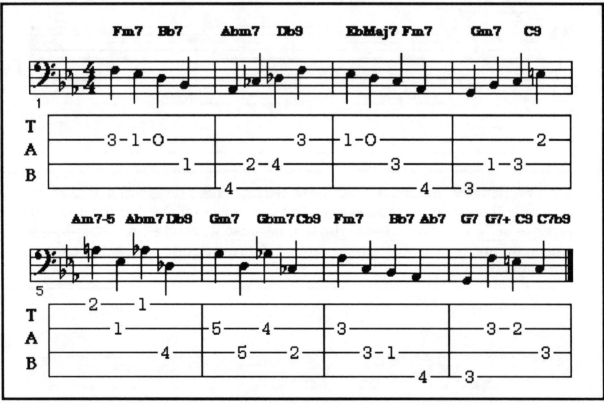

One very good way to improve your ability to create bass lines is to sit down with some books that contain old standards, preferably songs that you are not familiar with, and just read through the chord changes, making up the bass part to fit those chords. It is possible to learn many different variations on the same song using different rhythmic approaches and varying the use of chord tones.

TRANSPOSING ....

One last thing to talk about—**transposing** bass lines from one key into another. This means taking bass lines and/or ideas in one key and playing the same thing in another key. Many times you will be asked to play a song in a key that is different from the key in which you learned it.

Rather than being out of luck in that situation, it is helpful to know how to take a piece of music and *generalize* the chord progression by changing the chords to numbers. Then do the same with the notes in the bass line relative to the chords themselves. Now you can play the part in any other key, because you only need to think of that new key in terms of numbers, not necessarily note names.

Here are some examples of bass lines that get transposed into other keys. Identify the chords as numbers and the notes as numbers relative to the each chord.

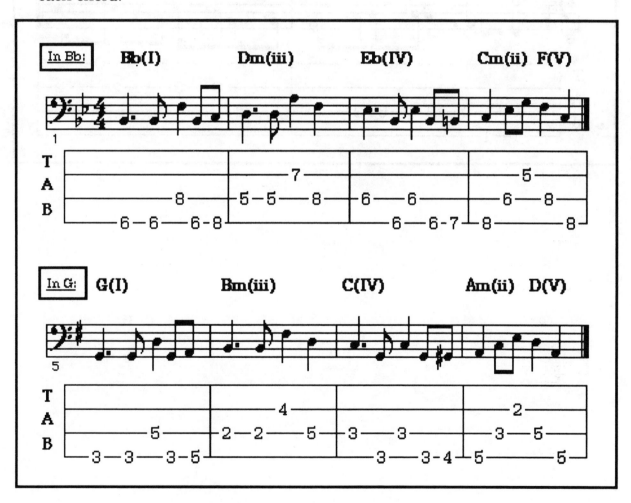

201

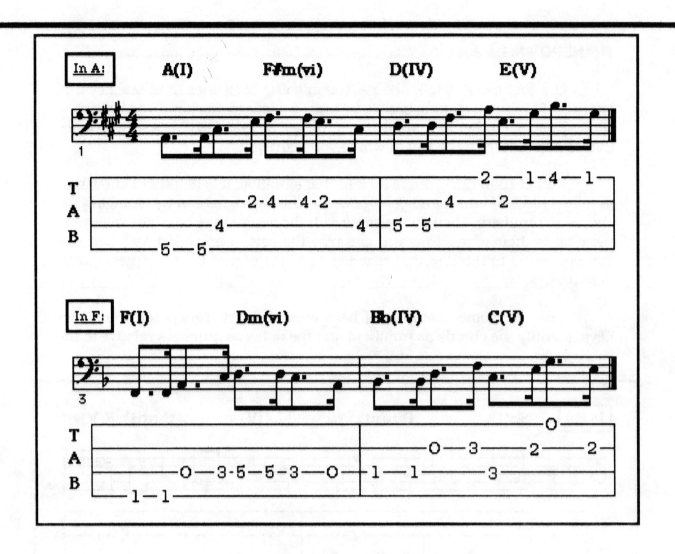

This last one is left for you to transpose into any key you like:

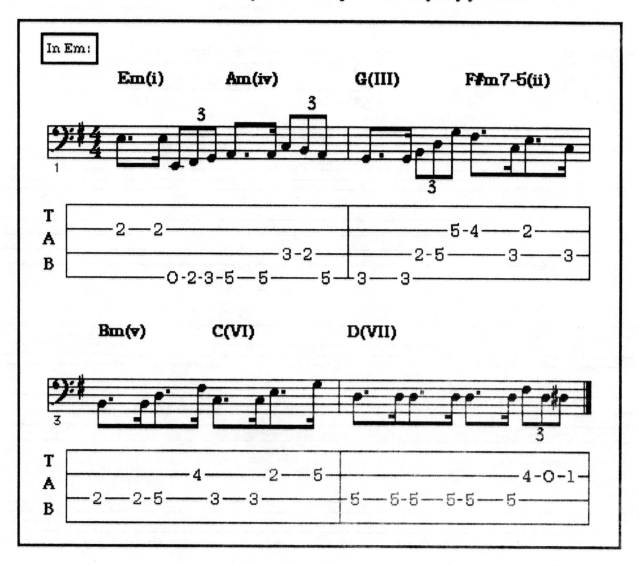

I hope that this book has been able to provide you with a bunch of information that will help improve your playing, and subsequently your enjoyment of playing the bass and making music. It doesn't matter if you're making a million dollars or a million cents at it—the important thing is that you're making music! *Have fun and good luck....*